JOY

TO THE

WORLD

Carrie & David Grant

Joy

TO THE

WORLD

Celebrating the stories behind the world's best-loved Christmas songs

LION

Published by Lion Books
Part of the SPCK Group
SPCK Group, Studio 101, The Record Hall, 16–16A Baldwin's Gardens,
London EC1N 7RJ, UK
www.spck.org.uk
ISBN 978-1-73941-783-3
eISBN 978-1-73941-784-0

10 9 8 7 6 5 4 3 2 1

First edition 2025

EU GPSR Authorised Representative
LOGOS EUROPE, 9 rue Nicolas Poussin, 17000, LA ROCHELLE, France
E-mail: Contact@logoseurope.eu

A catalogue record for this book is available from the British Library
Printed and bound in China by Dream Colour (Hong Kong)
Printing Ltd

Printed on paper from sustainable forests

Revd Carrie Grant MBE and **David Grant MBE** are BAFTA-award-winning broadcasters, vocal coaches, leadership coaches and pastors. Their TV and music careers have spanned more than 40 years; from having numerous hit records to appearing on BBC 1's *Fame Academy*, *Pop Idol*, *The One Show* and *Songs of Praise*. They have lived and breathed music their whole lives and have worked with many of the world's leading singers, musicians and songwriters. Carrie and David have been married for 37 years and have four children.

Contents

Preface

Part One
Songs from Long Ago

Part Two
Best-Loved Carols

Part Three

Holiday Songs

Part Four
Time to Party!

Part Five
Friends & Loved Ones

Part Six
Songs for the World

PREFACE

When we were approached to write this collection of wonderful Christmas songs, our first thought was, what a splendid opportunity. This was swiftly followed by the reality of the mammoth task of whittling it down to just sixty. There are some real corkers in here and there are also invariably some we have left out. Hopefully, we have captured the essence of the season from every angle; the spiritual, the sing-along, to pop favourites and the tear-jerkers.

Day after day we have found ourselves in the middle of a super-hot summer, dressed in shorts and T's while humming a Christmas tune or singing about sledging in snow and decorating trees on crisp winter evenings!

There is nothing to put you in the mood for Christmas more than the songs that have become the soundtrack of our lives, whether that be in church, at a family dinner, an office party or a shopping centre. This collection aims to give you a little potted history, a peppering of the Christmas magic and a little factual seasoning for the season.

We hope you enjoy!

Carrie and David

xx

PART
ONE

Songs from Long Ago

Coventry Carol

'COVENTRY CAROL' IS ONE OF THOSE CHRISTMAS TUNES that feels like it should come with a note saying, 'may cause seasonal melancholy'. Unlike the jolly carols that blare from shopping-centre speakers, this fourteenth-century English hymn is like an achingly beautiful but disturbing historical drama.

The carol's origins are rooted in the medieval mystery plays performed in Coventry, England, specifically, the 'Pageant of the Shearmen and Tailors'. This particular mystery play focuses on the Massacre of the Innocents, as King Herod, in a fit of paranoid rage, orders the execution of all male infants in Bethlehem. Mystery plays were hugely popular and were staged in various towns and cities around the country, and indeed across Europe. In fact, so popular and spectacular were the Coventry plays that it is recorded King Richard III came to see them.

The song's lullaby quality contrasts sharply with its grim subject matter, as if someone decided that the best way to deal with historical atrocity was to sing about it softly and soothingly. The haunting melody and the lyrics, 'Lully, Lullay, thou little tiny child', create an eerie juxtaposition, painting a picture of sorrow cloaked in the guise of a Christmas lullaby. There's a sense of resigned sadness; a reminder that the Christmas story has always contained its share of darkness. What's compelling about the 'Coventry Carol' is its ability to bring a historical reality into the celebrations. In a season often dominated by commercial excess, it provides a sombre counterpoint, forcing us to remember that the season's joy has always been tempered by the trials of the human condition.

Listening to the 'Coventry Carol' is a bit like finding a dark undercurrent in a sea of holiday fluff. It's a reminder that Christmas is also about acknowledging the profound and sometimes painful aspects of human experience. If you're in the mood for a Christmas carol with some historical gravitas, the 'Coventry Carol' will deliver.

Video

Deck the Halls with Boughs of Holly

'DECK THE HALLS WITH BOUGHS OF HOLLY' IS A CHRISTMAS song that has been sung and enjoyed for centuries. With its catchy melody and festive lyrics, this timeless tune has become synonymous with Christmas celebrations. It's an irrepressibly chipper Christmas carol, and a mandate to assault your home with greenery and garish decorations. Originating from a sixteenth-century Welsh air, 'Nos Galan', it's essentially the soundtrack for anyone who thinks a tasteful Christmas is an oxymoron.

While the melody was derived from a traditional Welsh winter carol, the original lyrics, which included references to drinking and general merrymaking were added by the Scottish musician Thomas Oliphant in 1862. The lyrics we know today first appeared in the Pennsylvania School Journal in 1877. Over time, the song's popularity spread, and it became a part of Christmas traditions worldwide.

The opening line, 'Deck the halls with boughs of holly', immediately sets a joyful and festive tone. The lyrics encourage the decoration of one's home with evergreen branches, symbolising the arrival of the Christmas season. The repetition of the word 'fa-la-la-la-la', adds a playful and rhythmic element to the song, making it a sing-along experience where you don't even have to know the lyrics to join in. As the carol progresses, it becomes

it's about celebration in its loudest, most colourful form

clear that 'Deck the Halls' is a kind of musical embodiment of the holiday spirit, but not the serene, candle-lit variety. No, this is boisterous, it's about celebration in its loudest, most colourful form, where subtlety is left out in the cold shivering next to a single undersized but tastefully decorated tree.

Yet, for all its bombast, 'Deck the Halls' serves an essential purpose. It's a reminder that Christmas, for all its religious significance and contemplative moments, is also a time for joy and exuberance. It's a season when even the most cynical among us can permit a bit of silliness, a touch of whimsy, and, yes, even an overdose of glitter. 'Deck the Halls' is a festive anthem for the part of Christmas that's unapologetically merry and bright. Sing it loudly, sing it badly, but most importantly, sing it with the kind of unrestrained joy that Christmas demands. Because sometimes, the best way to celebrate is to throw restraint and good taste to the wind and dive headfirst into a pile of tinsel and cheer a loud, 'fa-la-la-la-la!'

Video

Ding Dong Merrily on High

'DING DONG MERRILY ON HIGH' IS THE CAROL THAT brings a jolt of high-church pomp to any Yuletide gathering. If there's ever been a Christmas tune that screams, 'Look at me, I'm festive and sophisticated,' this is it. Forget about your 'Silent Nights' and 'Jingle Bells' – this one's got Latin refrains and enough choral exuberance to wake the dead.

The melody of this sixteenth-century earworm originally came from a French dance tune. That's right – a dance tune. So, while you're imagining snow-dusted cathedrals, 300 years ago, people from Paris to Marseille were probably kicking up their heels to this ditty. Then along came George Ratcliffe Woodward in 1924, who decided this melody needed some Christmas cheer and a hefty dose of ecclesiastical flair. Enter the famous, 'Gloria, hosanna in excelsis!', a line that rolls off the tongue like a Latin-class fever dream.

Singing 'Ding Dong Merrily on High' is like being thrust into the middle of a Christmas pageant. The verses chug along pleasantly enough, painting a picture of bells a-ringing and angels a-singing. But then comes the chorus, 'Gloria, hosanna in excelsis!'; a vocal Everest that demands you take a deep breath and hit notes higher than a kite on a windy day. It's not a carol for the faint of heart or the tone-deaf.

Yet, there's something endearingly chaotic about 'Ding Dong Merrily on High'. It's a carol that embraces the joyful noise of Christmas in all its unrefined glory. There are no solemn reflections or quiet moments here, just a full-throttle celebration that's part Renaissance fair, part Christmas knees-up, and entirely unapologetic in its unabashed and enthusiastic festivity.

This carol is a favourite with choirs and in festive gatherings, particularly those where someone insists on dragging everyone into a spirited sing-along. By the end of it, you're either filled with holiday cheer or hyperventilating while lying down in a darkened room in order to recover. It's a boisterous reminder that Christmas isn't just about quiet reflection – it's also about making a joyful noise. So, the next time 'Ding Dong Merrily on High' rings out, embrace it, take a deep breath and belt out that 'Gloria' with gusto.

Video

Gaudete

'GAUDETE' IS THE KIND OF CHRISTMAS CAROL THAT MAKES you feel like you've stumbled into a medieval Latin Mass. This sixteenth-century hymn is less about jingle bells and more about serious rejoicing: it is a stark reminder that Christmas wasn't always about eggnog and decorations, it had a touch of the dark, mystical and downright otherworldly.

The tune of 'Gaudete' was written by the sixteenth-century composer Arcadelt, for a poem called 'Vitam quae faciunt', which in turn is based on a setting of the same poem from 1534 by Senfl. 'New' words were then set to the existing tune. The fact that the whole carol is in Latin, makes it both charmingly archaic, and utterly baffling to most modern ears. It's as if the song insists, 'If you want to feel the true spirit of Christmas, you'd better brush up on your dead languages.' And yet, the chant-like melody has a way of getting under your skin. It's catchy in a haunting, primal sort of way. You can almost see the flickering candles and smell the incense. The refrain roughly translates to, 'Rejoice,

rejoice! Christ is born'. It's a stark reminder of the season's religious roots, devoid of the commercial fluff that clutters our modern celebrations.

'Gaudete' appeared in *Piae Cantiones*, a collection of sacred songs published in 1582. It's survived wars, plagues and centuries of cultural shifts. How many songs can you say that about? This carol is the great-great-grandparent of all Christmas music. There's something about its raw, unadorned simplicity that cuts through the tinsel and commercialism, bringing us back to a time when Christmas was about the profound mystery of faith.

this carol is the great-great-grandparent of all Christmas music

The song was popularised in 1972 when British folk group Steeleye Span had an a cappella hit with it. It is one of only two British hit singles to be sung entirely in Latin. 'Gaudete' isn't just a carol – it's a time machine. It's a blast from the medieval past that reminds us of the roots of our festive celebrations. It's a call to rejoice, in a way that's both ancient and, strangely enough, eternally relevant.

Video

God Rest Ye Merry, Gentlemen

'GOD REST YE MERRY, GENTLEMEN' IS THE CHRISTMAS carol that struts in with a confident swagger, offering festive cheer and a stiff upper lip. Written in England, an early version of this carol is found in an anonymous manuscript dating from the 1650s. The song is the musical equivalent of an old English pub where the ale is hearty, the fire is roaring and everyone is in good spirits, come what may. The term gentlemen would have applied to those who were of minor nobility, educated men, but despite this, they are those who would have to find their own work and make their own way in the world. It is suggested the night watchmen of the time sang 'God Rest Ye Merry, Gentlemen' as they walked the streets of London.

The opening lines, 'God rest ye merry, gentlemen, let nothing you dismay,' is basically saying, 'Hey, lads, keep your chins up!' It's a reassuring slap on the back, promising that all is well because the Saviour is born. This isn't some ethereal, floaty sentiment, it's practical advice wrapped in a jolly tune. The song is mentioned in Charles Dickens's *A Christmas Carol*, a clear indication that by the mid-1800s it was a Christmas staple.

> a reassuring slap on the back, promising that all is well because the Saviour is born

Musically, the tune is a no-frills affair. It's a robust, almost medieval melody that doesn't try to dazzle with orchestral pomp. Instead, it delivers its message with a sturdy rhythm that's perfect for a rousing sing-along. There's no glossy production here – just the raw, unvarnished spirit of an old carol that's seen it all.

The lyrics march through the nativity story with a brisk efficiency, 'Remember Christ our Saviour was born on Christmas Day, to save us all from Satan's power when we were gone astray.' It urges us to recognise that Christmas isn't just about presents and feasting, but about some serious theological heavy lifting. Its no-nonsense message cuts through the commercial noise, reminding us that, sometimes, the most meaningful part of Christmas isn't the glitz or the sparkle. 'God Rest Ye Merry, Gentlemen' stands apart from the flurry of modern Christmas music with its unpretentious simplicity and directness. It's not trying to sell you anything or make you feel warm and fuzzy; it's simply reminding you that the heart of Christmas can also lie in steadfastness and faith.

Video

15

I Saw Three Ships

'I SAW THREE SHIPS' IS THE CHRISTMAS CAROL THAT FEELS like it wandered in from a seaside pub, bringing with it a whiff of salt air and a pint of ale. This traditional English carol dates back to the seventeenth century, and it's got all the charm of an old sea shanty. If most carols are about snowscapes, bells and angelic visitations, this one's about maritime logistics and an apparent lack of geographic awareness.

In fact, it didn't even start as a Christmas carol. Historically carols used to be sung in all four seasons. The word comes from a French word *carole*, which was a popular circle dance. Consequently, the song 'I Saw Three Ships' was originally called, 'As I Sat On A Sunny Bank'.

The lyrics we sing today are from 1833, written by English lawyer William Sandys. They set up a scene that's both improbable and whimsical. The song doesn't bother explaining why there'd be three ships sailing into landlocked Bethlehem. Maybe they took a wrong turn at the Mediterranean and decided to dock anyway? Or perhaps it's just a poetic device, a nod to the idea of the Magi arriving by ship instead of camel, because, well, why not? It's Christmas – anything goes.

Musically, the carol has a jaunty, upbeat tune that's catchy, buoyant and carefree. Compared to the solemnity of many Christmas hymns, it's refreshing. It's more about celebrating the journey, no matter how historically inaccurate or geographically challenging that journey might be. What's delightful about this carol is its refusal to take itself too seriously. It doesn't bother with heavy theological themes or historical precision; it's just a festive romp that invites everyone to join in the fun. So what if three ships couldn't actually have sailed into Bethlehem? The song's invitation is to share a sense of joy and wonder that's as infectious as it is endearing.

'I Saw Three Ships' doesn't try to be profound, it's just a fun, light-hearted ditty. It's a carol that gladly embraces the whimsical and the joyful, and its enduring popularity proves that Christmas can be a time for both reverence and a bit of playful imagination.

Video

In Dulci Jubilo

'IN DULCI JUBILO' IS THE MEDIEVAL CHRISTMAS CAROL which brings a touch of Gothic exuberance to the holiday season. It's a song that feels like it should be sung in a candle-lit cathedral while contemplating the existential complexities of life in the Middle Ages. Written by German Dominican monk, preacher and writer Heinrich Seuse, at some time in the fourteenth century, this carol is a lively celebration of the birth of Christ.

The title itself, 'In Dulci Jubilo', translates to 'in sweet rejoicing', and Seuse's original lyrics mix Latin and Middle High German, creating a linguistic mashup that's as confusing as it is beautiful. Lines such as, 'In dulci jubilo [Latin], nun singet und seid froh! [German]', are both a call to joy and a reminder that, back in the day, before the printing press and the concept of everyone being able to read, people didn't bother much with language barriers when it came to praising the divine. Later Latin–English translations have been made by Percy Dearmer and Robert L. Pearsall.

The carol paints a picture of pure, unadulterated celebration. Dearmer's version of the first verse reads, 'Our hearts' joy lies in the manger; And it shines like the sun in the mother's lap.' It's an image straight out of a medieval nativity scene, complete with a golden-hued aura that practically glows with holiness. Forget the cold, hard realities of medieval life – plague, famine and feudal oppression, this is all about basking in the heavenly light of the newborn Christ.

this is all about basking in the heavenly light of the newborn Christ

Musically, *In Dulci Jubilo* is an intricate blend of soaring melodies and rich harmonies. It's the kind of piece that makes you feel like you're part of something much grander than yourself, like you're momentarily lifted out of your mundane existence into a realm of divine celebration.

The carol was introduced to many by Mike Oldfield with his 1975 instrumental cover that catapulted it into the realm of progressive rock. Oldfield, best known for *Tubular Bells*, decided to infuse the carol with a modern twist. The result was a blend of traditional festive spirit and contemporary musical innovation; a nod to both the past and the present. Oldfield managed to maintain the song's original jubilant essence while adding his signature style, making it both a respectful homage and a bold reinterpretation. Listening to Oldfield's 'In Dulci Jubilo' you're simultaneously in a medieval cathedral and a 1970s recording studio, experiencing the best of both worlds. It's a musical reminder that the spirit of Christmas can be both timeless and contemporary.

'In Dulci Jubilo' is a festive throwback to a time when celebrating Christmas meant you had survived another year and had something to sing about. It's a carol that captures the essence of medieval joy – simple, earnest and deeply rooted in faith.

Video

O Come, All Ye Faithful

THE ORIGINS OF 'O COME, ALL YE FAITHFUL' CAN BE traced back to the eighteenth century, although its exact beginnings are shrouded in some mystery. It's been attributed to various authors including King John IV of Portugal (1604–1656) and John Reading (1645–1692), who was Master of Choristers at Lincoln Cathedral, Chichester Cathedral and Winchester Cathedral. But despite many claimants, it is commonly believed to have been written by John Francis Wade, an English hymnist and music copyist. The hymn was originally written in Latin as, 'Adeste Fideles', and was published in the 1750s. It was not until 1841 that an English translation of the song was made by English Catholic priest Frederick Oakeley, allowing it to be sung and enjoyed by a wider audience.

The opening line, 'O come, all ye faithful, joyful and triumphant', sets the tone for the song, inviting everyone to come together in celebration and worship. The lyrics emphasise the themes of faith, unity and devotion, urging people everywhere to gather and adore the newborn Christ. Encouraging a sense of community and togetherness, the song reminds us of the importance of sharing in the joy of Christmas.

it's the kind of song that fills church pews, concert halls and raucous Christmas sing-alongs

The melody is majestic and stirring, perfectly complementing the anthemic lyrics. Beginning with a simple and solemn introduction, it gradually builds in intensity as the verses progress. The chorus, 'O come, let us adore him', which is repeated three times, also builds in volume and intensity and is a powerful call demanding participation.

The carol's beauty lies in its blend of the majestic and the intimate. The music swells with a kind of royal grandeur, fitting for the arrival of a king, but it also carries a personal, almost cosy undertone. It's like throwing a royal ball in your living room; it's grand and regal but at the same time warm and inviting.

The song isn't just about theological reverence; it's also about community and collective joy. It's the kind of song that fills church pews, concert halls and raucous Christmas sing-alongs with a sense of shared experience.

In a world that often feels divided, 'Oh Come, All Ye Faithful' reminds us of the power of gathering together, setting aside our differences and focusing on the true meaning of Christmas. It's a reminder of the joy and hope that Christmas can bring, encouraging us to approach Christmas with a spirit of love, gratitude and reverence. It invites us all to be part of something bigger, even if just for the duration of a song.

Video

O Come, O Come, Emmanuel

'O COME, O COME, EMMANUEL' IS THE PERFECT Christmas carol for those who find joy in the dark, melancholic corners of the holiday season. It's the sonic equivalent of a Gothic cathedral at dusk – solemn, haunting, and deeply evocative. This hymn, with roots tracing back to the eighth century, brings an almost medieval gravity to the season's musical lexicon.

Unlike some of its more jubilant counterparts, 'O Come, O Come, Emmanuel' doesn't try to plaster a grin on your face, it dives straight into the spiritual yearning and existential angst that often get buried. The song's minor key and plaintive melody carry an ancient weight. The carol is a plea for deliverance, 'O come, O come, Emmanuel, and ransom captive Israel'. This isn't your average Christmas wish list; it's a cry for salvation from a people in exile, yearning for divine intervention, a reminder that Christmas wasn't always about consumerism and sparkle. It was, and for many still is, a profound celebration of hope amid despair.

In a world where Christmas has been hijacked by commercialism and the relentless pursuit of happiness, 'O Come, O Come, Emmanuel' is a refreshing dose of reality. It acknowledges that the season isn't just about joy and light; it's also about waiting, hoping and sometimes feeling a little lost. It's a carol for those who find themselves staring out at the falling snow, pondering the state of their soul while the rest of the world sings about reindeer and mistletoe. The carol's lyrics, translated from the original Latin in 1851, are a direct appeal for divine intervention, a cry for deliverance from a world seemingly shrouded in darkness. They are more of a desperate plea than a festive greeting, resonating with anyone who's ever felt the heavy burden of waiting for better times. The melody's Gregorian chant origins lend it an austere beauty, stripping away the gloss and getting to the raw, unvarnished heart of Christmas.

'O Come, O Come, Emmanuel' is a breath of fresh, albeit chilly, air. It's a reminder that the festive season is as much about introspection and the hope for redemption as it is about merrymaking. The sombre strains of this ancient hymn remind us that even in the darkest times, there's a flicker of hope to be found.

Video

O Tannenbaum (O Christmas Tree)

'O TANNENBAUM', THE HOLIDAY CAROL THAT SINGS THE praises of the Christmas tree with such sincerity that it might make you want to hug a tree – not in a sickly-sweet way, but in a 'thanks-for-the-memories' kind of way. Because this isn't just a song – it's a love letter to the steadfast evergreen, a symbol of reliability in a season sometimes heavily marked by chaos and consumerism.

The roots of 'O Tannenbaum' dig deep into the cultural soil of sixteenth-century Germany. The melody came from a folk song, and the modern lyrics were penned in 1824 by Ernst Anschütz, a Leipzig organist who decided that trees deserved more recognition than just being considered as seasonal decorations. Originally, it wasn't even a Christmas carol, but a song of ill-fated love. It wasn't meant to describe a Christmas tree or the act of decorating a Christmas tree, it was written as a tribute to the tree's steadfastness, its evergreen nature symbolising enduring life, faithfulness and dependability. Anschütz added new verses and it eventually became associated with Christmas.

Imagine yourself in a cosy, wood-panelled tavern in Germany, the air thick with the aroma of mulled wine and the hum of conversation. Suddenly, someone strikes up 'O Tannenbaum' and the room joins in, each verse a toast to the tree's unwavering greenery. 'O Tannenbaum, O Tannenbaum, wie treu sind deine Blätter!', a line that roughly translates to, 'O fir tree, o fir tree, how faithful are your needles'! It's a moment of communal appreciation, a reminder that amid the seasonal frenzy, some things remain steadfast, consistent and dependable.

Fast-forward a few centuries, and 'O Tannenbaum' has gone international, morphing into, 'O Christmas Tree' in English-speaking lands. Admittedly, the lyrics have been tweaked to better fit the festive cheer, but the essence is unchanged. It's about celebrating the tree's quiet strength and unchanging beauty, representing a stark contrast to the ephemeral glitz of modern Christmas lights and decorations.

Video

The First Noel

'THE FIRST NOEL' IS A TRADITIONAL ENGLISH CAROL WITH Cornish origins. It was originally, and in the UK often still is, entitled 'The First Nowell', Nowell being an early English synonym for 'Christmas' from the French Noël, meaning the Christmas season. The word was regularly used in carols from the Middle Ages to the late 1800s. 'The First Noel' is one of those timeless Christmas carols that reminds us of simpler times when a star in the sky was breaking news. Originating in England in the sixteenth or seventeenth century, this song has an endearing, straightforward charm.

The carol starts with, 'The first Noel, the angel did say, was to certain poor shepherds in fields as they lay.' You get the sense that this isn't just a carol, but a scene setter. It's like the opening of *Star Wars*, but instead of a galaxy far, far away, we're transported to the pastoral fields of Bethlehem. The shepherds are not just bystanders; they are the unlikely

*

recipients of the divine memo about the birth of Christ. It's like getting front-row seats to the biggest event in history, and all you had to do was show up for work.

Although the origins of 'The First Noel' can be traced back to the sixteenth or seventeenth century, the song was not transcribed until 1823, when it was published in London as part of an early anthology called *Some Ancient Christmas Carols*. It is believed to have been passed down through oral tradition before being written down and published. The carol features a simple melody, making it easy for people to sing along to. It's an inescapable part of the Christmas soundtrack and can be heard pretty much everywhere throughout the season.

'The First Noel' has been recorded by numerous artists and has in this century alone been a hit on the US Billboard Christmas charts by four different artists. What makes 'The First Noel' so enduring beyond its musical appeal, is that it's a beautiful reminder of the joy and wonder that surround the birth of Jesus. Its unpretentious delivery invites us to embrace the Christmas message. It doesn't get bogged down in poetic flourishes. It just tells it like it is – a straightforward recounting of the nativity that feels like a warm, familiar story told by a grandparent sitting by the fireside. In a world that often feels complicated, 'The First Noel' is refreshingly straightforward. It's melodic comfort food for the soul, a nostalgic return to a simpler time when all you needed to celebrate Christmas was a star, some shepherds and a song.

Video

The Holly and the Ivy

'THE HOLLY AND THE IVY' IS THE KIND OF CHRISTMAS CAROL that makes you think an amateur botanist got their hands on a hymnal. Written in the 1800s in England, it's less about the joy of the season and more about the joy of foliage. If you've ever wanted a lesson on the symbolic significance of common plants set to music, this is for you. It paints a picture of Christmas that is more forested than festive.

The song starts with a pastoral image, 'The holly and the ivy, when they are both full grown'. It's as if the Victorians decided to lecture us on landscaping. Nobody knows exactly the reason that holly and ivy became associated with Christmas, although as they are both common native and decorative evergreens it's not an unreasonable choice, what we do know is that from medieval times holly and ivy become symbolic of the season. Holly, with its jagged leaves and red berries, symbolised Jesus' crown of thorns and the blood of his sacrifice. Ivy, on the other hand, represented either his mother Mary or eternal life. Whatever the origins, the lyrics are certainly a deep dive into the world of plants-as-religious-metaphors. The holly tree 'bears the crown' and 'bears the berry', while the ivy is there, alongside, to keep the holly company.

Musically, it's a gentle tune, beloved in the musical world. The carol originally had a variety of melodies, but the version that is sung worldwide today was collected in 1909 by the English folk song collector Cecil Sharp in the Gloucestershire town of Chipping Campden in England.

According to Sylvester, who included the carol in his 1861 collection named *A Garland of Christmas Carols*, the song was first published in 1710, and thereafter lay dormant and overlooked for around 150 years. What's fascinating about the song is its staying power. It's a reminder that our Christmas traditions have roots (pun intended) that go far deeper than plastic trees and LED lights. This carol connects us to the natural world, hinting that the sacred and the secular, the eternal and the seasonal, have long been intertwined.

In the end, 'The Holly and the Ivy' is more than just a carol – it's a lesson in how to find the divine in the mundane. It's a reminder that even in the dead of winter, life goes on. Perhaps also a reminder of the quiet, enduring beauty of nature.

Video

PART TWO

Best-Loved Carols

Angels from the Realms of Glory

'ANGELS FROM THE REALMS OF GLORY' COMBINES
heavenly grandeur with a call to action. Written by James
Montgomery in 1816, this hymn has been ringing through
church halls and carol services for over two centuries.
Montgomery, whose missionary parents died in the West
Indies when he was still in school, was a Scottish newspaper
editor and equality campaigner. He used his newspaper, the
Sheffield Iris, to campaign for the abolition of slavery and
to draw attention to the hardships endured by boy chimney
sweeps. His commitment to inclusion and equality can be
clearly heard in the carol's lyrics. It's not just a song; it's a
proclamation, summoning everyone, from shepherds to
sages, to witness the miracle of Christmas.

it's a proclamation, summoning everyone ... to witness the miracle of Christmas

Think of it as the nineteenth-century equivalent of a blockbuster movie trailer, complete with a star-studded celestial cast. The opening line, 'Angels from the realms of glory, wing your flight o'er all the earth', sets the stage for a divine spectacle. It's like the heavenly host is the ultimate PR team, spreading the word far and wide, inviting all to 'come and worship' the newborn king. It's an inclusive call to action, making it clear that this is an event no one should miss, and everyone's got an invitation.

What's striking about 'Angels from the Realms of Glory' is its blend of high theology and down-to-earth accessibility. The song moves from the mundane, 'Shepherds in the fields abiding', to the celestial, 'God with man is now residing', covering all bases. Almost as if it's reminding you that, yes, angels are involved, but so are you. There's an urgency to the call: 'Come and worship, come and worship, worship Christ, the newborn King'. It's not a suggestion; it's a commandment dressed up in joyous exclamation.

It's a song that transcends time and space, inviting everyone to partake in the Christmas story. The grandeur of the angels contrasts beautifully with the humility of the manger scene, creating a compelling narrative arc. It's a reminder that Christmas is not just a cosy, fireside holiday but a cosmic event with universal implications.

The carol was sung to a variety of tunes until 1928, when in the UK the Oxford Book of Carols set it to the beautiful French tune 'Iris' (*Les anges dans nos champagnes*), which proved to be its perfect setting. 'Angels from the Realms of Glory' is a call to remember the spiritual significance of the season, a reminder that beyond the tinsel and lights lies a story of divine intervention and human hope. And an announcement that no matter who we are, there's a place for us all in the Christmas story.

Video

Away in a Manger

'AWAY IN A MANGER' IS ONE OF THE MOST-LOVED
Christmas carols in the world, especially for children. It
is a gentle and tender lullaby that celebrates the birth of
Jesus and the humble surroundings in which he was born.
The lyrics of the carol evoke a sense of peace and awe. But
who wrote those lyrics? It's a musical mystery worth further
investigation.

The carol is believed to have originated in the late
nineteenth century and was at first described as a
translation of a song by Martin Luther, the famous German
theologian and reformer. In fact, until the twentieth century
it was called 'Luther's Cradle Song'. Historians have since
debunked this theory, as none of Luther's writings mention
the song, and no German text for the carol has been found
from earlier than 1934, more than fifty years after the first
English-language publication. The melody and the words

of the first two verses were actually written in America in the 1880s and the third verse was added later. 'Away in a Manger' also has two popular musical settings, one regularly sung in the US, the other better known in the UK and Ireland.

The melody most familiar in the UK, known as 'Cradle Song', is thought to have originally been composed by Jonathan Spilman in 1837, later adapted in 1895 by William Kirkpatrick. 'Mueller' is the melody best known in the US, it was penned by James Murray and first published in 1887 as part of a musical collection called *Dainty Songs for Little Lads and Lasses*.

Lyrically, the first verse of the carol sets the scene of the nativity, describing a peaceful and serene environment, 'Away in a manger, no crib for a bed, the little Lord Jesus laid down his sweet head'. These words remind us of the simplicity and humility of Jesus' birth, despite his divine nature. Yet, for all its simplicity, 'Away in a Manger' has staying power. It's been sung by everyone from Sunday-school choirs to famous artists, each bringing their own spin to this tender tableau. The song's enduring appeal lies in its universal themes of innocence, humility and divine love. It's a gentle reminder that Christmas isn't just about the hustle and bustle; it's also about quiet moments of reflection and awe.

'Away in a Manger' is a reminder that sometimes the simplest stories are the most powerful. It's a carol that whispers rather than shouts, inviting us to find the sacred in simplicity and the divine in the everyday.

Video

Hark! The Herald Angels Sing

ALTHOUGH IT'S A HUGELY POPULAR CHRISTMAS CAROL, 'Hark! The Herald Angels Sing' has proven to be something of a festive shape-shifter, taking a number of forms before becoming the carol that we know today. Behind it all is the story of the many people who contributed to its creation.

In 1739 Charles Wesley, the English clergyman and hymn writer, penned a poetic hymn titled 'Hark, How all the Welkin Rings' as part of a collection called *Hymns and Sacred Poems*. Welkin means sky or heaven, and the hymn was filled with exuberant praise about the birth of Jesus, celebrating the message of peace and goodwill. However, the song didn't really catch on or become particularly popular in its original form. Fourteen years later, in 1753, George Whitefield, a prominent preacher and friend of Charles Wesley, adapted and revised it. Among the lyrical changes Whitefield's version included the famous opening line, 'Hark! The herald angels sing', which instantly captured the attention of its listeners.

However, it was a hundred years later that the hymn truly gained its musical identity. In 1840, the renowned composer, Felix Mendelssohn, composed a cantata entitled 'Festgesang' to commemorate the 400th anniversary of Johannes Gutenberg's invention of the printing press. And fifteen years later, in

Wesley's evocative lyrics read like a theological manifesto

1855, a transformative moment occurred when English musician and organist, William H. Cummings decided to combine Wesley's lyrics, with Whitefield's opening line and Mendelssohn's melody. Cummings made some alterations to the tune to fit the words, and voilà – the song we know today was born.

The popularity of 'Hark! The Herald Angels Sing' soared, and it became a recognised part of Christmas celebrations worldwide. Wesley's evocative lyrics read like a theological manifesto, packed with doctrinal declarations. Phrases like, 'God and sinners reconciled', and 'glory to the newborn King' aren't just festive window dressing. It's as if Wesley

40

decided that the best way to celebrate the birth of Christ was to cram an entire theology course into three minutes of song.

In today's holiday landscape, 'Hark! The Herald Angels Sing' can feel like an anachronism; it's unapologetically serious about its subject matter. While modern Christmas music sometimes leans into sentimentality, this carol stands as a reminder of the holiday's more solemn origins. And goodness knows, sometimes we all need a little bombastic glory.

'Hark! The Herald Angels Sing' is stately, grand and slightly out of place amid the consumerist frenzy of today. Yet, that's precisely what makes it enduring. It pulls us back to something more profound. It's a call to pause and to reflect on the miraculous rather than the materialistic.

Video

In the Bleak Midwinter

IF YOU ARE LOOKING FOR A CHRISTMAS CAROL THAT strips away the gaudy tinsel and glitter, leaving just the raw, unadorned reality of a cold, hard winter then 'In the Bleak Midwinter' is the one for you. It is the Christmas carol that brings a dose of sobering, chilly realism to the otherwise jolly season. Penned by English poet Christina Rossetti in 1872, and later set to music by Gustav Holst and Harold Darke, this hymn presents a refreshingly austere take on the holiday season.

a hauntingly poignant reminder that even in the bleakest of times, there's a reason to hope

Rossetti's poem starts with an acknowledgment of the harshness of winter, 'In the bleak midwinter, frosty wind made moan, Earth stood hard as iron, water like a

stone,' This isn't your picturesque, snow-dusted postcard; it's the brutal truth of winter at its most unforgiving. Rossetti serves it up cold, reminding us that winter is often more about survival than celebration. It's more Siberian wasteland than winter wonderland. It's about the harsh reality of a season that in many places tests the limits of human endurance. Rossetti's poetry is stark and unflinching, painting a picture of a world frozen in time and space, where warmth is a distant memory.

Yet, amid this desolation, the flame of hope flickers. The carol moves from the stark portrayal of the natural world to the warmth of the nativity scene, 'Our God, heaven cannot hold him, nor earth sustain; Heaven and earth shall flee away when he comes to reign,' It juxtaposes the unforgiving environment with the miraculous birth, a cosmic event taking place in the humblest of settings. It's a nod to the profound truth that light can indeed pierce through the darkest of winters.

Musically, the carol's sombre, haunting melody underscores its themes of hardship and hope. It's not designed for merriment; it's meant for contemplation. It invites you to stare out into a snowstorm and reflect on Christmas's deeper meanings. It asks the question, what gift should we bring to the God-child, and concludes that the only thing worthy of such a saviour as this is to give one's heart.

'In the Bleak Midwinter' is the perfect antidote to the relentless and sometimes artificial cheer of a modern

Christmas. It acknowledges that the season can be harsh and unforgiving, yet still manages to find a glimmer of divine light amid the gloom. It's a hauntingly poignant reminder that even in the bleakest of times, there's a reason to hope.

Video

It Came Upon the Midnight Clear

'IT CAME UPON THE MIDNIGHT CLEAR' IS THE CHRISTMAS carol that marries Victorian idealism with an almost naive optimism about human nature. Penned in 1849 by a pastor named Edmund Sears, the hymn paints a picture of peace on earth brought about by celestial intervention. It's a Christmas carol that asks us to believe, however briefly, in a world that's far kinder than our own.

The opening lines set the scene with typical Victorian flair: 'It came upon the midnight clear, that glorious song of old, from angels bending near the earth to touch their harps of gold.'

A lovely image to be sure, but let's inject a bit of reality here. Picture angels, daintily plucking their golden harps over a world where people are slogging through Victorian-era filth, political unrest and industrial grime. The angels might be singing, but the folks down below are probably too preoccupied with more immediate concerns like avoiding cholera or finding their next meal.

Sears then implores us to, 'rest beside the weary road and hear the angels sing'. It's a noble idea, suggesting we take a break from our frantic pace to soak in some divine harmony. But the reality is that most people were too busy navigating their own 'weary roads' to pause for angelic background music. The roads remain weary, and the people remain oblivious, caught up in the minutiae of survival.

Musically, the carol is serene and uplifting; its gentle melody perfectly designed to make you forget, for a moment, the world's harsh realities. It's the auditory equivalent of a warm blanket on a cold night, fostering a fleeting sense of solace and goodwill. 'It Came Upon the Midnight Clear' is the quintessential Victorian dream, that of universal harmony. It's a sweet, almost naive call to imagine what our world would look like if divine intervention broke into our day-to-day chaos. As such, it feels both nostalgic and eerily relevant. Its plea for peace and reflection

it's the auditory equivalent of a warm blanket on a cold night

seems as urgent now as it did in Sears's time. While the shopping centres and airwaves are filled with songs pushing merriment to the point of mania, this carol offers a chance to step back and breathe; to remember what Christmas is supposed to be about.

Video

Joy to the World

'JOY TO THE WORLD' IS THE CHRISTMAS CAROL THAT
declares, in no uncertain terms, that the holiday season
is here to bulldoze over any lingering gloom. Written by
minister, theologian and hymn writer Isaac Watts in 1719,
with music later adapted from Handel by Lowell Mason,
it's the kind of hymn that doesn't just usher in the season
– it blasts it through the front door with a fanfare and a
bullhorn. If Christmas cheer were a sporting event, this
carol would be the undisputed champion. It's joyous, it's
triumphant, and it has absolutely no time for any Scrooge-
like cynicism.

The opening line, 'Joy to the world, the Lord is come!' is a
full-throated declaration that something monumental has
happened. It's not a gentle nudge; it's headline news, it's a
cosmic announcement. Forget the dreary realities of daily
life, the King has arrived, and you'd better get on board

with the celebration. Watts is essentially bellowing, 'Stop what you're doing and get excited!' The lyrics don't so much invite you to revel in the moment as they demand it, with a confidence that suggests Watts was less a humble hymn writer and more an evangelist for unrestrained spiritual exuberance.

The carol continues with, 'Let earth receive her King; Let every heart prepare him room, and heaven and nature sing.' It's an unrelenting call to universal rejoicing. No exceptions. Even heaven and nature are in on it too, harmonising in a grand celestial chorus.

Musically, Mason's arrangement gives us a piece that's robust and jubilant. It's no coincidence that this carol often gets the full choral and orchestral treatment. It's meant to be big and bold; a musical reminder that this is a time for unrestrained joy.

'Joy to the World' is the ultimate anthem of Christmas celebration. It doesn't just suggest that you be joyful; it practically shouts in your ear, 'The celebrations have begun, what are you waiting for?' It's a forceful reminder that, despite the stresses and strains, Christmas is ultimately about unbridled joy. It's a call to rejoice in the good news of the season, loudly and without reservation.

Video

Mary, Did You Know?

warm, fuzzy feelings of Christmas and gives them a gentle, thought-provoking shake. Written by Mark Lowry with music by Buddy Greene, this modern carol has become as much a part of the Yuletide landscape as overcrowded shops and mince pies. But let's not kid ourselves: it's no 'Jingle Bells'. This is Christmas with a dash of existential inquiry.

In 1984 Mark Lowry scribbled down some questions that had popped into his head about the nativity. He wasn't just thinking about shepherds and wise men. No, Lowry went straight for the jugular, asking Mary if she had any inkling that her baby boy would one day be the superstar of miracles. Then Buddy Greene came along in 1991, slapped on a melody, and a classic was born.

The song's questions are the kind of queries that would give any new parent pause for thought. Most are not asked on the maternity ward if they expect their children to 'one day walk on water'. I can almost see Mary raising an eyebrow and saying, 'Well, that wasn't exactly in the, *What to Expect When You're Expecting Handbook.'* It's an interrogation wrapped in a lullaby, probing the divine mystery with all the subtlety of a nosy neighbour.

Uniquely among popular Christmas songs, every line of the song's three verses poses a question. This pattern is only punctuated by the middle section's declaration of some of the miracles Mary's baby will perform.

'Mary, Did You Know?' is the singers' song and has been covered by everyone from country crooners to pop divas. Cee-Lo Green had a hit with it and Pentatonix got in on the action, turning the song into an a cappella sensation. It's often the song choice of great singers performing over Christmas.

'Mary, Did You Know?' is a reminder that the Christmas story is not just about the manger and the star. It's not just about the birth of a child; it's about the beginning of a life that would reshape the world. So, this Christmas, while we're navigating the holiday chaos, let's spare a thought for Mary. Not only did she face the trials of new motherhood in less-than-ideal conditions, but she also had to contemplate the cosmic significance of her son's future. It's a tall order, and this song captures that weight with a poignancy that's hard to ignore. It serves as a reminder that behind the festive cheer lies a story of the most profound significance.

Video

O Holy Night

'O HOLY NIGHT' IS THE CHRISTMAS CAROL EQUIVALENT of a fine French wine – rich, complex and more than a little intoxicating. Penned originally in French in 1843 by Placide Cappeau, a poet who fittingly also sold wine, with music composed in 1847 by Adolphe Adam. It's a song that has become a cornerstone of our Christmas soundscape.

rich, complex and more than a little intoxicating

It's considered a classic for several reasons. First, the carol's lyrics beautifully capture the essence of the nativity scene and its deeper meaning. The song's poetic and heartfelt words resonate with people of all ages and backgrounds, connecting with the spiritual and emotional significance of Christmas.

Second, the melody of 'O Holy Night' is both enchanting and powerful, with the music perfectly complementing the lyrics and evoking a sense of wonder and joy, and by the time it reaches its climactic high note, it's demanding every ounce of attention, turning even the most jaded listener into an unwilling participant in a moment of sublime beauty.

Additionally, 'O Holy Night' has a universal message of hope, peace, redemption and liberation. The latter contributed to the song eliciting a fair share of controversy before the abolition of slavery. The third verse features the lyrics, 'Chains shall he break, for the slave is our brother, And in his name all oppression shall cease'. In the United States this made the words popular among abolitionists in the north and unpopular among the slave owners of the south. The lyrical focus on shared humanity and humility, 'fall on your knees', was highly controversial to some in the 1840s and 1850s, as many believed enslaved people to be less than human. A later source of controversy was the discovery that Cappeau, the lyricist, was an atheist and rumours that the composer Adolph Adam was Jewish. This caused the carol to be declared unfit for church services in some places.

But over time the song took on a life of its own, gaining in popularity with each passing generation, its timeless message resonating across continents and cultures. Because 'O Holy Night' isn't just about the music, it's about the sense of something greater than the sum of our usual holiday excesses. It reminds us that Christmas is meant to be a time of awe and wonder, not just a festival of conspicuous consumption. It brings us back to the essence of the season – a flicker of hope, a whisper of peace and a promise of redemption, all packed into a few minutes of sonic grandeur.

Video

O Little Town of Bethlehem

'O LITTLE TOWN OF BETHLEHEM' IS A BELOVED CHRISTMAS carol that poignantly captures the serene and sacred atmosphere of Bethlehem on the night of Jesus' birth. The lyrics were written by Phillips Brooks, an Episcopalian priest, in 1868, and the original music to the US version of the carol was composed by his church organist, Lewis H. Redner. Brooks was inspired to write the song after visiting Bethlehem in 1865. In the UK, the carol is usually sung to the tune 'Forest Green', which was adapted from an English folk ballad by Ralph Vaughan Williams and first published in 1906.

The carol paints a tranquil and reverent picture of Bethlehem on a night like no other. The opening lines, 'O little town of Bethlehem, how still we see thee lie', set the scene, highlighting the town's quiet and calm as it unknowingly hosts one of history's most significant events. The song reflects on the songwriter's sense of the humble surroundings and the miraculous nature of Christ's birth, detailing how in the stillness of the night, beneath a canopy of stars that whispered secrets to the earth, on this night, this holy night, something extraordinary was unfolding.

'O Little Town of Bethlehem' is less about the actual geography of Bethlehem and more about the geography of the heart

What makes 'O Little Town of Bethlehem' enduring is its ability to transport us back to this idealised version of Christmas. It's not about historical accuracy; it's about capturing the essence of the Christmas spirit – a moment of quiet reflection amid the chaos. So, while the real Bethlehem might have been far from silent that night, Brooks's carol offers a respite, a chance to imagine that, just for a moment, the world could be as peaceful and perfect as his lyrics suggest.

Cliff Richard's 1982 take, the truncated 'Little Town', with a completely new scan of the lyrics to a new melody and rhythm deserves mention here as an excellent version. Written by Chris Eaton, it was also a success in the USA when covered by Amy Grant in 1983 on her, 'A Christmas Album'. It has been taken up in many church settings, where this version as well as the traditional versions of the song are sung.

When approaching this carol, it's essential to realise that 'O Little Town of Bethlehem' is less about the actual geography of Bethlehem and more about the geography of the heart. It's a reminder that, amid the noise and clutter of modern life, there's still room for a bit of quiet wonder. It's a sweet, if somewhat sanitised, vision of what Christmas could be, if only we could all just pause and listen.

Video

Once in Royal David's City

'ONCE IN ROYAL DAVID'S CITY' WALKS THE FINE LINE between nostalgia and reverence. In choral form it usually opens with a solitary, pure soprano voice – and there's something angelic about that first verse sung solo. This deeply traditional Christmas carol holds a special place in the hearts of many. 'How traditional?' you may ask. Well this carol, written as a poem by Cecil Frances Alexander in 1848, and set to music a year later by the organist Henry Gauntlett, is the song that opens the Festival of Nine Lessons and Carols, the annual Christmas Eve service at King's College Chapel, Cambridge.

'Once in Royal David's City' was originally in a collection of poems called *Hymns for Little Children, to be sung in Sunday Schools or at home*. Other well-known songs from the collection include, 'All Things Bright and Beautiful', and 'There Is a Green Hill Far Away'.

The opening line transports the listener back in time to the humble town of Bethlehem, where the story of Jesus' birth unfolds. The verses introduce us to the central characters of the nativity story, Mary and the baby Jesus. The lyrics not only invite us to imagine ourselves in the stable witnessing the miracle of Christmas, they also make us realise the Victorians could turn anything – up to and including the birth of the Messiah – into a stiffly formalised ritual. As the song progresses, we are not only taken on a journey through the events surrounding the birth of Christ but also reminded of the expectations placed on Victorian children, with the less than subtle message, 'Christian children all must be mild, obedient, good as he'. In penning this, Cecil Frances Alexander didn't just want to celebrate Christmas – she took the opportunity to weaponise it as a tool of behavioural correction.

But the real beauty of 'Once in Royal David's City' lies in how it balances its simplicity with its message. It's not only about the nativity scene or children's behaviour; it's about the ideal of innocence and humility, virtues that are often forgotten.

It's also a subtle reminder of the universality of the Christmas story. By starting small – a single voice, a single town – it builds to a powerful crescendo, involving the whole choir and congregation. It's as if the song itself is saying, 'We all have a part in this' and that's the charm of it. 'Once in Royal David's City' brings us back to the simple enduring truth of Christmas – that something wonderful and hopeful can begin in the most humble of places.

Video

Silent Night

'SILENT NIGHT' IS THE QUINTESSENTIAL CHRISTMAS carol that wraps the gritty reality of the nativity in a soft, comforting blanket of peace and calm. Nevertheless, it has a strong claim to being the world's most popular Christmas carol, as it is by far the most recorded of all time. The music was written in 1818, by Franz Xaver Gruber and the lyrics by Joseph Mohr, later translated into English in 1863 by John Freeman Young. This hymn paints an idyllic picture of a serene and holy night, which, let's be honest, is probably a far cry from what actually happened in that Bethlehem stable.

'Silent night, holy night! All is calm, all is bright' – of course it was, if you ignore the pungent aroma of livestock, the frantic anxiety of new parents, and the chaotic aftermath of childbirth. There's no mention of Mary's exhaustion or Joseph's probable bewilderment as he tried to figure out how to care for a newborn amid the clamour of animals. Instead, we get this pristine image of celestial calm. The carol's lyrics paint a picture of perfect stillness, 'Round yon virgin, mother and child! Holy infant so tender and mild'. It's an image straight out of a Renaissance painting with halos and peaceful smiles.

The melody is simple, almost hypnotic, designed to lull you into a state of reflective peace. No bombast here, no jingle bells or rockabilly riffs – just a gentle tune that feels like a lullaby for a weary world. In today's relentless drive for more – more gifts, more parties, more Instagram-worthy moments, 'Silent Night' is the antithesis of excess. It's the song that asks you to pause, to step away from the hustle and bustle, and to find a sliver of peace amid the madness. It's the musical equivalent of turning off the glaring Christmas lights and letting the natural beauty of a winter night take over.

The song is often used in church carol services at the magical moment when the lights go down and Christingle or other candles are lit. There is a stillness to the song that can be felt. It is also a choir favourite as it lends itself to many different arrangements with various harmonies and countermelodies.

'Silent Night' is a carol that epitomises the idealism of Christmas. It invites us to momentarily suspend our disbelief, to pause and imagine a world where the most chaotic events can be swathed in divine tranquillity.

Video

We Three Kings

'WE THREE KINGS' TRACES THE JOURNEY OF THE THREE
wise men, or Magi, to find the baby Jesus. The song has a
rich history and has become a familiar part of the Christmas
musical tradition. It was written by John Henry Hopkins Jr
in 1857. He was the rector of a church in Pennsylvania and
wrote the carol for a Christmas pageant in New York City.
It is noteworthy that Hopkins composed both the lyrics and
music, when at the time carol composers usually wrote
one or the other, but only rarely both. Although written
in 1857, Hopkins didn't publish the carol until 1863 when
he published his book, *Carols, Hymns, and Songs*. 'We
Three Kings' was the first Christmas carol originating from
the United States to achieve widespread international
popularity. *The Oxford Book of Carols* published in 1928,
praised the song as, 'one of the most successful of modern
composed carols'.

From the outset, with the proclamation, 'We three kings of Orient are', the song establishes the sense of a grand, far-reaching quest. These men, often depicted as bearing gifts of gold, frankincense and myrrh, are not just travellers; they are bearers of profoundly symbolic offerings. Gold represents Jesus' kingship, frankincense his divinity, and myrrh his mortality. These gifts, though seemingly impractical for a newborn, are deeply laden with spiritual significance.

'We Three Kings' is known for its haunting melody and evocative lyrics, which transport listeners to the scene of Jesus' birth and capture the sense of awe and wonder that the wise men must have felt as they embarked on their journey to honour the newborn King. It's often sung as part of the Christmas Eve or Epiphany services, commemorating the visit of the Magi.

The journey the wise men embarked upon is central to the carol, reflecting themes of guidance, faith and perseverance. The star they follow is a beacon, a symbol of celestial guidance leading them through deserts and over mountains.

'We Three Kings' has been recorded by countless artists and has been both adapted and parodied in various arrangements. The song endures because it encapsulates a fundamental essence of the Christmas story – the recognition of a divine event by learned men from distant lands, the convergence of different cultures in a humble setting, and the universal quest for spiritual truth.

Video

PART THREE

Holiday Songs

Carol of the Bells

'CAROL OF THE BELLS' IS THE KIND OF CHRISTMAS CAROL that feels like it should come with a health warning: 'May cause intense feelings of Christmas urgency'. 'Carol of the Bells' is based on the Ukrainian New Year's song, *'Shchedryk'*. The music was written by Ukrainian composer Mykola Leontovych in 1914 and the English lyrics were written by Peter Wilhousky in 1936.

The 'Carol of the Bells' is about as far from 'Silent Night' as you can get. If most carols gently nudge you into the Christmas spirit, 'Carol of the Bells' slaps you across the face with jingle bells aplenty.

The song's frenetic pace and cascading melody sound like a Yuletide alarm clock. From the moment those four notes start their relentless ringing; you know you're in for something that's going to make you feel like you're running late for Christmas. It's not so much a carol as it is an aural caffeine shot, designed to jolt even the most laid-back listener into a state of festive hyperactivity.

The lyrics, when they finally join in, are a rapid-fire celebration of bells heralding the season. In short staccato phrases the 'sweet silver bells' urge us to 'throw cares away'. Yes, it's a nice sentiment, but the breathless delivery makes it feel less like advice and more like a command from some manic festive dictator.

And maybe that's exactly why it's become such a staple of the seasonal soundtrack, heard everywhere from commercials, to movies, to shopping centres. It encapsulates the frenetic pace of the modern Christmas season, where the joy of the holiday is matched only by the frenzy of preparations. There's no time to sit around, there are gifts to buy, parties to attend and trees to decorate.

In the midst of it all, 'Carol of the Bells' is brilliant precisely because it's a bit unhinged. It captures the chaotic joy and the urgent excitement of the season. Amid the calm, cosy moments of Christmas, it's a reminder that for many it's the whirlwind of activity that makes this time of year so exhilarating. In a world where we're constantly told to slow down and savour the moment, this carol gives us permission to embrace the madness with open arms. And sometimes, a little bit of that wild, festive energy is exactly what we need.

Video

Do You Hear What I Hear?

'DO YOU HEAR WHAT I HEAR?' IS THE CHRISTMAS CAROL that turns the nativity story into a full-blown auditory extravaganza. The song was written in 1962 by Noël Regney and Gloria Shayne Baker, who would jointly and separately write many other hits, among them, 'Rain, Rain Go Away' for Bobby Darin, 'Almost There' for Andy Williams, and 'Dominique' for The Singing Nun. They infused this carol with a sense of high drama. It's like the Christmas equivalent of a blockbuster film trailer – epic, dramatic, and unrelenting in its quest to grab your attention.

The song starts with a plaintive question from the night wind to the little lamb and quickly escalates into a full-blown celestial announcement. It's as if the night wind, in a fit of poetic zeal, decided to drop a major revelation about the birth of Jesus. The carol's structure is a bit like a relay race, with each verse passing the message from one character to another, culminating in a climactic call to action. First, it's the night wind and the little lamb, then the shepherd and the mighty king, all trying to outdo each other in relaying the great news.

Musically, 'Do You Hear What I Hear?' comes replete with dramatic rises and falls that are designed to ensure that you're not just hearing the message; you're feeling it. It has a big, sweeping melody that sounds like it was lifted straight from a Broadway musical or a prime-time Christmas special. The orchestration is lush, making sure every note resonates with the sort of grandeur the song's lyrics demand. What's interesting about the song is its ability to capture both the simplicity of the nativity story and the grandeur of its retelling. It manages to communicate that what happened on this quiet night in Bethlehem was an event of cosmic significance, all within the span of a few verses.

'Do You Hear What I Hear?' is more than just a carol; it's a reminder that Christmas can be as dramatic as it is joyful. It focuses our attention squarely on the nativity, in doing so it ensures that the message isn't just heard but felt.

Video

Have Yourself a Merry Little Christmas

THE SONG 'HAVE YOURSELF A MERRY LITTLE CHRISTMAS' is an absolute A-list Christmas classic. It was written by Hugh Martin and Ralph Blane and premiered in the 1944 MGM musical *Meet Me in St Louis*, starring Judy Garland. The song has since become an anthem, evoking feelings of warmth, loss, joy, sadness, poignancy and nostalgia.

The film of *Meet Me in St Louis* tells the story of a year in the life of a family living in the early 1900s. As part of the film's narrative, they needed a half-happy, half-sad song

to capture the bittersweet emotions of the characters during the Christmas season. Hugh Martin, who is credited with the lyrics, initially wrote a set of melancholic and downbeat lyrics for the song, which Judy Garland felt were too depressing, so she requested a more uplifting and hopeful version. Martin rewrote the lyrics, and the result was the now famous, 'Have Yourself a Merry Little Christmas'.

The revised lyrics still acknowledge the hardships and challenges of life but offer a message of hope and togetherness. The song encourages listeners to cherish the present moment, even in the face of an uncertain future. 'Have Yourself a Merry Little Christmas' is an honest acknowledgment of life's imperfections. It accepts that not everything is wrapped up neatly with a bow. Words like, 'if the fates allow' and 'we'll have to muddle through, somehow', acknowledge that life doesn't always go as planned. It's the Christmas song for realists, the ones who know that sometimes the best you can do is to make the most of the moment you're in.

However, the Christmas classic was close to never being written. Hugh Martin reportedly said, '"Have Yourself a Merry Little Christmas" began with the melody. I found a little madrigal-like tune that I liked but couldn't make work, so I played it for two or three days and then threw it in the wastebasket.' But co-writer Blane told Martin that the song was too good to throw away. 'We dug around the wastebasket and found it,' Blane said, 'Thank the Lord we found it.'

Thank the Lord indeed, as since its debut, 'Have Yourself a Merry Little Christmas' has been recorded by numerous artists, and Frank Sinatra, Michael Bublé, Josh Grobin, Keysha Cole, Sam Smith and John Legend are among those that have had a hit with the song.

its enduring appeal lies in its ability to evoke a sense of warmth without sugar-coating reality

Its enduring appeal lies in its ability to evoke a sense of warmth without sugar-coating reality. It's like a comforting presence offering a moment of reflection and encapsulating the emotions of many.

Video

It's Beginning to Look a Lot Like Christmas

WRITTEN BY MEREDITH WILLSON IN 1951, 'IT'S BEGINNING to Look a Lot Like Christmas' is a hugely popular Christmas song, capturing the essence and excitement of the Christmas season. When first released by Perry Como in September 1951 and then by Bing Crosby just a few weeks later, 'It's Beginning to Look a Lot Like Christmas' was an instant hit for both. There is a belief that Willson wrote the song while he was resident at Yarmouth's Grand Hotel in Nova Scotia, Canada, as the lyrics mention a 'tree in the Grand Hotel' and 'one in the park' too. Yarmouth's Frost Park is directly opposite the Grand Hotel. There is a further reference to a store called 'The Five and Ten', which was also in Yarmouth at the time the song was written.

It's a song that transports listeners into a world filled with festive cheer and anticipation, painting a vivid picture of the sights and sounds that signal the arrival of Christmas. From the iconic images of 'toys in every store', to the mention of candy canes and 'silver lanes aglow', the song beautifully captures the visual transformation that takes place at this magical time of year.

the song beautifully captures the visual transformation that takes place at this magical time of year

The song evokes a sense of joy and excitement as it describes the activity and preparations that come with Christmas. It celebrates the tradition of decorating homes and streets with lights and ornaments, in an effort to create a welcoming, happy atmosphere. The lyrics also mention the joyful anticipation of receiving gifts, as children eagerly await Santa's arrival on Christmas Eve.

'It's Beginning to Look a Lot Like Christmas' also carries a deeper message of togetherness and love, reminding us of the importance of spending time with loved ones at Christmas. The song encourages us to cherish and appreciate the moments of connection and joy that the season brings.

Over the years, 'It's Beginning to Look a Lot Like Christmas' has been covered by numerous artists, most successfully in the twenty-first century by Michael Bublé, who had a

Top 10 hit with the song in more than twenty-five countries worldwide, further cementing its status as a holiday classic. It has also been used widely in film, most notably in *Home Alone 2: Lost in New York* and the children's classic, *Polar Express*.

'It's Beginning to Look a Lot Like Christmas' encapsulates the spirit of the holiday season. Whether it's played on the radio, sung by carollers, or just playing in the background, its cheerful melody and nostalgic lyrics continue to spread cheer and bring people together year after year.

Video

It's the Most Wonderful Time of the Year

'IT'S THE MOST WONDERFUL TIME OF THE YEAR' – THE anthem of Yuletide optimism. It was written for *The Andy Williams Christmas Show* in 1963, and his seasonally excited crooning has been pumping out of radio, TV and shopping-centre speakers every December since.

It's a sugar-coated classic promising us a season full of joy, warmth and togetherness, a vision so wholesome it's practically dripping with saccharine nostalgia. Straight out of a Norman Rockwell painting, the song paints a picture of a magical winter wonderland, where families gather for 'gay happy meetings', with hearts glowing. This ditty asserts the holiday season as a nonstop parade of innocent joy, punctuated by 'carolling out in the snow'. Of course, back in 1963, they also thought smoking was good for you and seatbelts were optional, so forgive us if we're just a little sceptical.

it's a sugar-coated classic promising us a season full of joy, warmth and togetherness

Let's break it down. The song croons about 'kids jingle belling', as if children spend their December days politely ringing bells. No sign of children spending their days hyped up on candy canes and threatening to destroy the house unless you buy them the latest overpriced, plastic, landfill-bound toy. Most children spend December systematically dismantling your will to live by demanding presents so absurdly specific they make a NASA project look like a straightforward task. Meanwhile, most parents are mainlining coffee to survive the shopping centre, which has transformed into a capitalist mosh pit where people will trample you to death for a discount on a waffle maker. Oh the realities of the season!

Then the song waxes lyrical about 'parties for hosting', with little thought of being cornered by a distant relative who reeks of red wine and regret, and wants to explain his latest conspiracy theory, while you nod and wonder if there's a polite way to flee. It even has the audacity to claim there will be 'scary ghost stories'. In reality, the most you'll hear is Uncle Bob's tale of almost dying in a Costco car park. Scary, yes – but not quite in the way Andy Williams intended.

And yet, for all this, 'It's the Most Wonderful Time of the Year' has become an established, welcome and loved part of the seasonal playlist. It has been used in Christmas commercials by numerous large national and multinational retail groups and has featured in the UK and US December charts for the last two decades, becoming more popular and successful with each passing year. So raise a glass, assume the recovery position and press play.

Video

Let It Snow!
Let It Snow!
Let It Snow!

'LET IT SNOW! LET IT SNOW! LET IT SNOW!' IS A CLASSIC winter song that has become synonymous with the festive season, despite not ever mentioning Christmas. It is the quintessential winter anthem for anyone who prefers their snowflakes seen through the window of a warm, cosy living room, rather than while shovelling a garden path. Written in 1945 by lyricist Sammy Cahn and composer Jule Styne, the song was actually penned during a sweltering summer, proving once again that nothing inspires thoughts of winter wonderlands like an oppressive heatwave. It was recorded that year by singer Vaughn Monroe and was a Christmas hit. Despite no reference to the season, it has since become totally associated with Christmas

The song's lyrics depict a cosy, idyllic scene of a couple enjoying each other's company indoors while a snowstorm rages outside. It begins by establishing a contrast between the warm, comforting 'delightful' interior and the cold, harsh, 'frightful' conditions outside. This juxtaposition is central to the song's charm, as it celebrates the comfort and intimacy found in spending time inside with loved ones during inclement weather. It is a sentiment anyone who's ever dealt with a blizzard can get behind. This is not just a song; it's a manifesto for the winter-weary. It says, 'Why brave the elements when you can sit by the fire with a glass of something warm?'

'Let It Snow!' captures the essence of wintertime romance, with its gentle melody and repetitive chorus enhancing the sense of cosiness and contentment. Over the decades, 'Let It Snow!' has been covered by numerous artists, each bringing their own unique flavour to the song. Apart from the 1945 version by Vaughn Monroe, Dean Martin, Frank Sinatra and more contemporary artists like Michael Bublé have all had success with the song. Each rendition captures the song's timeless appeal, contemporising it and making the song a perennial favourite with successive generations.

'Let It Snow' is a charming ode to the pleasures of being snowed in, a tribute to the joy of doing nothing in the best company, and a celebration of a cold snowy winter, from a safe, warm distance.

Video

Sleigh Ride

'SLEIGH RIDE' EMBODIES THE FROTHY, FESTIVE SPIRIT OF the season. It's like a frosty breath of winter air sneaking through a crack in the window. The kind of tune that shows up everywhere and is more ubiquitous than a Santa at a shopping centre ... and it's just as unavoidable. It barrels into the holiday season like a snowball fight – sudden, chaotic, and irresistibly fun. Written by Leroy Anderson in 1948, it's a frenetic jaunt through a winter wonderland, wrapped up in an irresistibly catchy tune. Unlike carols that try to instil a sense of peace and reflection, 'Sleigh Ride' is all about the thrill of the ride, the crack of the whip, and the jingle of the bells.

Picture a snowy village, the kind that exists mostly in greeting cards. 'Sleigh Ride', with its lively orchestral arrangement, its rosy-cheeked charm and promise of snow-dusted romance, is the musical equivalent of that snow-covered picture. The lyrics, added later by Mitchell Parish, are a cascade of winter clichés: it's as if someone distilled every Christmas movie ever made into a single, relentless burst of cheer. There's no room for holiday blues here, just an unwavering push toward festive joy.

Despite, or perhaps because of its relentless optimism, 'Sleigh Ride' has been covered by countless artists but it's the Ronettes rendition that is the most played by modern audiences. Their version bursts like a confetti cannon – loud, colourful, and impossible to ignore. Recorded in 1963 and drenched in Phil Spector's 'Wall of Sound', it takes an already jaunty tune and raises it to the next level. Led by Ronnie Spector's iconic voice, The Ronettes dive into the song with a mix of sugar-coated sweetness and rock 'n' roll swagger.

Phil Spector's production is a symphonic assault on the senses, not so much over the top, more 'Is there a top?' Every second is filled with a cacophony of bells, strings and percussion, layered so densely that it's like trying to untangle a box of Christmas lights that's been shoved in the attic since last year. But that's the point – 'Sleigh Ride' isn't about nuance; it's about overwhelming you with festive cheer. The very core of the song is dripping with the kind of Yuletide bonhomie that makes it a celebration of winter wonder.

Video

The Christmas Song

'THE CHRISTMAS SONG' ALSO KNOWN AS, 'CHESTNUTS Roasting on an Open Fire', has become synonymous with icy winter nights and warm family gatherings. It was written in 1945 by Robert Wells and singer Mel Tormé,known as the 'Velvet Fog'. It has been recorded and performed by numerous artists. Although Tormé was a successful and accomplished singer, as soon as the song was finished, he took it to Nat King Cole, as he felt that it would be perfect for him. He was right. It is Nat King Cole's iconic rendition that has truly captured the hearts of listeners around the world. The song is an ode to seasonal cheer that never seems to get old. Like Christmas decorations from the attic, it's wheeled out every December. It's a beautifully crafted, pleasant and familiar version of an idealised Christmas.

Rather oddly, the song was born during a Los Angeles heatwave, and it didn't actually start as a song at all. In an effort to stay cool by thinking cool, this song, which would go on to become the most performed Christmas song in the world, was born. Mel Tormé recalled seeing a spiral pad on Robert Wells's piano with four lines written in pencil. They started 'Chestnuts roasting ... Jack Frost nipping ... Yuletide carols ... Folks dressed up like Eskimoes'. Tormé explained that Bob just thought if he could immerse himself in winter he might cool off. Within less than an hour, the song was written.

Nat King Cole's smooth and velvety voice, combined with the nostalgia and warmth of the lyrics create a magical and enchanting experience. Nat King Cole's interpretation of 'The Christmas Song' is marked by his impeccable phrasing and heartfelt delivery. His rich and soulful voice effortlessly captures the essence of the song, infusing it with warmth and emotion. As he sings about, 'tiny tots with their eyes all aglow', listeners are transported back to memories of their own childhood wonder at Christmas

The song has become a part of Christmas traditions around the world, and its timeless appeal transcends generations. The lyrics of 'The Christmas Song', combined with Nat King Cole's unforgettable voice, create a sense of nostalgia and warmth that captures the essence of Christmas.

Video

Walking in the Air

'WALKING IN THE AIR' IS A SONG THAT SHOULDN'T WORK but somehow does. From the 1982 animated film classic *The Snowman*, it's the kind of song that reminds you why the British shouldn't be allowed near Christmas. It's got that cold, dreary quality that only a nation which invented the stiff upper lip could produce. Forget about cheerful carolling or chestnuts roasting by the fire – this is Christmas for people who think seasonal joy is a vulgar American concept.

The song itself was originally sung by a St Paul's Cathedral choirboy, Peter Auty, who was 13 years old at the time. His voice is so pure it makes you wonder if he's been locked in a church since birth. It's haunting, in that 'innocence lost' sort of way, which is ironic because the whole thing is about a kid flying around with a snowman. A magical, life-affirming adventure, right? Well, no. Because in true British fashion, it's actually a metaphor for the fleeting happiness of youth,

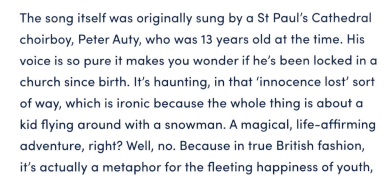

the impermanence of joy and – spoiler alert – the fact that the snowman melts at the end.

And in keeping with the story this child's voice is eerie, like he's already seen the crushing disappointment adulthood has waiting for us. Two years later in 1985 it began the now four-decades-long career of a then 15-year-old chorister named Aled Jones, when his version of the song was a Christmas hit in the UK. 'Walking in the Air' isn't really a Christmas song in the sugary, jingling sense. It's more like the musical equivalent of staring into the void while your aged aunt harangues you about life choices over Christmas dinner.

The strange thing is how well it all works. The lyrics are simple and sparse, yet somehow, they make you feel like you, too, are floating above a cold, indifferent world, insulated only by the ethereal tones of a prepubescent vocalist and the futile magic of snow. The music sweeps in like a winter storm, beautiful but unforgiving. It taps into that small, secret part of us all that still wants to believe in something magical. It is the song's melancholy that imbues it with a strange kind of magic. It's like staring into a snow globe and realising that all the happiness inside is temporary. But for three minutes, you get to float along with it, above the darkness and drudgery of everyday life. All in all, 'Walking in the Air' is probably the closest thing to seasonal existentialism you're going to get without having a drink with Nietzsche.

Video

White Christmas

'WHITE CHRISTMAS' IS CONSIDERED BY MANY TO BE the twentieth century's greatest contribution to Christmas music. Written by Irving Berlin and first performed by Bing Crosby in 1942 in the movie *Holiday Inn*, this timeless tune captures the nostalgia and longing for a traditional Northern Hemisphere, snowy Christmas.

The opening lines which picture a white Christmas 'just like the ones I used to know', instantly transport some of us to a place of security and familiarity, evoking images of snow-covered landscapes, twinkling lights and cosy gatherings. The song taps into our collective memories and yearnings for a picture-perfect Christmas.

Irving Berlin would often stay up all night writing and after completing this song, legend has it that he asked his secretary to take down the song saying that not only was it the best song he ever wrote, but it was the best song anybody ever wrote.

It's certainly the most successful song ever. Bing Crosby's version has sold well over 50 million copies, a world record, and when sales of all the versions of this song are added up, it's sold over 100 million copies.

originally released at the height of the Second World War, it conjured up nostalgic images

'White Christmas' has also had a significant cultural impact, not just in becoming the best-selling single of all time, but also earning an Oscar for Best Original Song. The song's popularity then led to the creation of a film of the same name, starring Bing Crosby himself. The movie, released in 1954, further cemented the song's status as a Christmas classic.

'White Christmas' has been covered by countless artists over the years, each bringing their own interpretation and style to the song. From orchestral renditions to contemporary pop versions, the song has been adapted to suit different musical genres and tastes. This versatility is a testament to its timeless appeal.

Originally released at the height of the Second World War, it conjured up nostalgic images of snowflakes falling gently, families gathering around a crackling fire, and the joy of being in the safety and familiarity of home together with loved ones. This tapped into the collective yearning for a simple and idyllic, war-free Christmas.

The song is still magical today. It reminds us of the power of music to touch our emotions and transport us to a different time and place. Whether we experience a white Christmas or not, the song is a symbol of the enchantment and beauty of Christmas, reminding us to cherish our memories and hold dear the traditions that bring us joy.

Video

Winter Wonderland

'WINTER WONDERLAND' IS A SONG THAT SOMEHOW successfully manages to sell the concept of a hard winter, which, let's be honest, is an impressive feat. Yet this song has been tricking people into feeling nostalgic about frozen misery since 1934, and you've got to admire that kind of optimism.

The genius of 'Winter Wonderland' is that it doesn't bother with reality – it's pure escapism, and that's exactly what the songwriters, musician Felix Bernard and lyricist Richard Bernhard Smith intended it to be. It's been recorded by over 200 artists and been a hit for many of them including Guy Lombardo, Johnny Mathis, Perry Como, The Eurythmics, Chloe and Laufey, whose 2023 version was the highest ever charting version of the song in Canada, Ireland and the United Kingdom.

'Winter Wonderland' doesn't care about your frostbitten toes or your car that won't start because the engine's frozen solid. No, it paints a picture of winter as it ideally should be – soft, glistening snow, the kind that reflects sunlight just enough to make you momentarily forget that you're losing feeling in your fingers and toes. It's a song where sleigh bells ring, snow is pristine and you actually want to go outside.

There's something deeply charming about the song's description of building a snowman in the meadow. It doesn't mention the mess or the cold, just the simple, childlike joy of stacking snow into something that briefly stands before collapsing in on itself. In a later 1947 version of the lyrics the snowman, originally called 'Parson Brown' became a 'Circus Clown', both versions are used in subsequent recordings. And the song's romantic vibe? It's brilliant. Forget about the dreary, grey reality of winter. In 'Winter Wonderland', you're holding hands with your sweetheart, dreaming by the fire, and not at all worried about slipping on ice and cracking a rib.

What makes 'Winter Wonderland' work is that it offers a version of winter where everything sparkles, everyone's in love, and even the snowman is invested in your happiness. It's a beautiful illusion, which ignores the fact that real winter involves power outages, frozen pipes and slipping on ice in front of your neighbour. But it's an illusion we're all happy to believe, at least for the few minutes that the song is playing, and there's absolutely nothing wrong with that.

Video

PART
FOUR

Time to Party!

Frosty the Snowman

'FROSTY THE SNOWMAN' IS THE WINTER DITTY THAT captures the whimsical side of Christmas, but let's face it – if you really think about it, it's more like a bizarre fever dream than a festive tale. Written by Jack Rollins and Steve Nelson in 1950, this jaunty tune tells the story of a snowman who magically comes to life, runs amok and then melts away, leaving kids with a memory and probably a need for therapy.

Picture it: a group of bored and frostbitten children, cobble together a snowman from whatever frozen slush they can scrape together. Suddenly, thanks to an old silk hat, this icy figure springs to life. And what does this newfound sentient being do? Does he reflect on the miracle of existence or the fleeting nature of life? No, he starts cavorting around town, acting like a snow-covered Pied Piper.

The lyrics are all fun and games, Frosty the snowman is 'a jolly, happy soul'. But there's an underlying absurdity to the whole scenario. Here we have a walking, talking snowman whose first instinct is to lead children on a wild, joyous romp. Frosty's antics are pure, carefree fun until, inevitably, he starts to melt. It's a stark reminder that all good things are fleeting, wrapped in a jingle that's meant to make you smile.

Musically, it's a jaunty, upbeat tune that makes you want to tap your toes. Although heavily played at Christmas time, Christmas itself is never mentioned in the lyrics. The song has been covered by many artists including Jimmy Durante, Nat King Cole and Guy Lombardo. The best-known, most-played version is the Phil Spector-produced 1963 version by The Ronettes, which features in *Rolling Stone*'s list of, 'The Greatest Rock & Roll Christmas Songs'.

'Frosty the Snowman' is a quintessentially quirky winter story, blending childlike wonder with a hint of existential dread; a 'live for the moment' anthem. So, next time you sing along, spare a thought for Frosty, the snowman who lived fast, played hard and melted away, leaving behind nothing but a puddle, a legend and a promise that he would be 'back again someday'.

Video

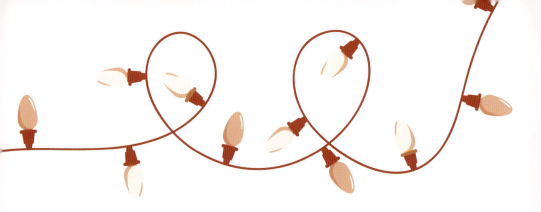

I Wish It Could Be Christmas Everyday

'I WISH IT COULD BE CHRISTMAS EVERYDAY' IS ONE OF those songs that takes the concept of Christmas cheer and dials it up to eleven. Released by Wizzard in 1973, it's a musical sugar rush, meant to transport you to a perpetual Yuletide utopia, a never-ending snow globe of festive joy. As for Christmas songs that could be sung on the football stands, this song is certainly up there.

Written by Wizzard frontman and ELO founder Roy Wood, the lyrics are a technicolour dream of Christmas perfection:

children building snowmen in the streets, sleigh bells ringing, and the unending goodwill of carollers. Wood isn't just describing a holiday scene; he's practically daring you to resist the allure of an eternal Christmas. It's a sentiment that feels almost rebellious in its exuberance, and that's precisely the point. Wood is giving us a vision of the festive season that's not just joyous but almost deliriously so.

Musically, the song is a 'Wall of Sound' that Phil Spector would envy, with blaring brass, jingling bells and a children's choir that tugs at your heartstrings. The backing vocals were by the Suedettes and a children's choir composed of 11- and 12-year-olds from Stockland Green School in Birmingham, who were bussed down to the studio in London. Wood wanted a festive feel and because the song was recorded in August, the air conditioning in the studio was turned down to its lowest setting possible and engineer Steve Brown hung up Christmas decorations in the studio. Clearly this worked because the song has become a Christmas perennial. Peaking at number 4 in the UK chart on initial release, it's since become a constant presence in the December charts, being in the Top 25 every year since 2011.

this song taps into a deep-seated desire to prolong the magic of the season

This song taps into a deep-seated desire to prolong the magic of the season. It's about wanting to hold onto that fleeting sense of wonder and warmth, to escape the mundanity of life a little longer. Wood's creation is pure escapism, a reminder that the essence of Christmas, beyond its overtly commercialised and sometimes glittering absurdity, is something worth dreaming about. So, turn up the volume, let the festive spirit wash over you, and for a moment, pretend the world really could be this jolly every day. Merry Christmas, eternally.

Video

Jingle Bell Rock

'JINGLE BELL ROCK' IS A SEASONAL EARWORM; THE KIND that attaches itself to your brainstem sometime around Halloween and won't let go until January. Written by Joe Beal and Jim Boothe in 1957, it's a kitschy blend of rockabilly and holiday cheer, designed to make you tap your toes. It's a song that refuses to settle into the background like elevator music. Since its debut in 1957, sung by Bobby Helms, it has barrelled through the season with all the subtlety of Santa falling down a chimney. This isn't just another Christmas tune; it's a rockabilly juggernaut that combines twanging guitars, upbeat rhythms and a relentless demand that you tap your feet and join in the merriment.

From the opening guitar riff, 'Jingle Bell Rock' sets the tone, Helms croons about 'jingle bell time' being a 'swell time', and you can almost see the poodle skirts and leather jackets swirling and swaying. This isn't about quiet reflection or solemn hymns – this is about hitting the dance floor and forgetting for a few minutes that winter can be a bleak, cold slog through slush and traffic jams.

The song's charm lies in its simplicity and infectious energy. It's as if it took the classic Christmas imagery, sprinkled it with some rock 'n' roll pixie dust, and created a tune that's as enduring as it is irresistible. There's no heavy lifting required here, no deep pondering about the meaning of the season, just pure, unadulterated fun. Today it's the perfect soundtrack for consumerism's high holy days, blaring from shopping-precinct speakers and office parties, forcing a smile to your face while you trudge through your Christmas shopping list.

Yet 'Jingle Bell Rock' has a certain perverse charm. The song doesn't aspire to be high art; it's there to inject a dose of innocent cheer into the darkest days of winter, and it does its job admirably. It's a throwback to a simpler era, a little Rockabilly tonic for Christmas lovers. But the real genius of 'Jingle Bell Rock' lies in its ability to transcend taste. You don't have to like it; it's there to be experienced. And despite its inherent cheesiness, there's something warmly endearing about it.

Video

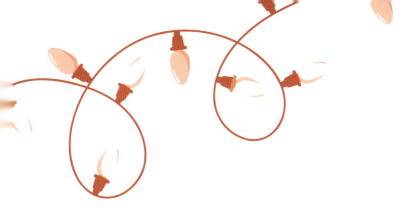

Jingle Bells

IN THE ANNALS OF CHRISTMAS MUSIC, FEW MELODIES have been embraced by successive generations with such warmth and ubiquity as 'Jingle Bells'. Originally penned by James Lord Pierpont in 1850, it was initially called 'The One Horse Open Sleigh'. Although it is said that it was originally conceived as a Thanksgiving song, it has since become a symbol of Christmas cheer and merriment. Its relentless optimism and sheer catchiness transcend religious and cultural boundaries, captivating listeners of all backgrounds and beliefs.

The opening lines of the first verse, 'Dashing through the snow, in a one-horse open sleigh', paint a picture of Victorian-era thrill-seeking. This isn't your average Christmas carol; it's more like the nineteenth-century version of a winter F1 race, complete with the potential for chaos and mishaps. The sleigh ride described isn't just a leisurely trot; it's an exhilarating, wind-in-your-face, freeze-your-extremities adventure. In an example of masterful storytelling, the lyrics suggest a carefree, almost reckless spirit, weaving a tale of anticipation and joy that comes with being untethered from daily responsibilities – just you, the snow, and a horse that hopefully knows the way home.

Yet beneath its seemingly simple facade, 'Jingle Bells' carries subtle shades of nostalgia and longing. As the lyrics unfold, we are transported to a bygone era, where horse-drawn carriages were a common mode of transportation and the jingling of bells echoed through the wintry air. Gore Vidal, the renowned American author and essayist, reputedly once remarked, 'Jingle Bells possesses a unique ability to conjure a collective memory, bridging the gap between past and present.'

a testament to the power of music to create a sense of sentimental yearning for a time the listener never knew

Beyond its melodic and nostalgic allure, 'Jingle Bells' also serves as a testament to the power of music to create a sense of sentimental yearning for a time the listener never knew. This isn't a song that contemplates the deeper meanings of Christmas; it's about pure, unadulterated fun. It's a reminder that the holiday season isn't just about quiet reflection and cosy firesides; it's also about braving the elements and maybe having a good laugh when things go hilariously awry.

'Jingle Bells' is bold and boisterous, inviting you to sing along; in fact it practically dares you not to. This isn't a mere Christmas tune, it's practically a cultural touchstone and a rowdy reminder that in the middle of winter there's always room for laughter and cheer.

Video

Mary's Boy Child (Oh My Lord)

'MARY'S BOY CHILD' IS THAT RARE BREED OF CHRISTMAS song – a calypso-infused carol that manages to weave together festive cheer, theological gravitas and a toe-tapping beat. Written in 1956 by Jester Hairston, an African-American composer, conductor and choir leader, who was also considered the leading authority on black spirituals. Alongside 'Amen', a hit for Curtis Mayfield and the Impressions, 'Mary's Boy Child' is his most famous composition. This tune is a theological cocktail, blending the sacred and secular in a way that's unconventional, yet delightful.

Picture this: it's the mid 1950s, and Hairston, a man whose name sounds like he should be selling you high-end grooming products, pens a song that retells the nativity story. But instead of the sombre tones of a traditional carol, he opts for the lively rhythms of calypso – a musical genre more often associated with palm trees and sunny beaches than stables and mangers. The result? A song that feels like a Christmas party in the Caribbean, with just a hint of theological reflection to keep it grounded.

The opening lines beginning, 'Long time ago in Bethlehem' set the scene with all the gravitas of a biblical epic narrated by your uncle who's had a bit too much sherry. Yet it works, the simplicity of the lyrics captures the essence of the nativity story without getting bogged down in the kind of overwrought sentimentality that often plagues Christmas music.

The chorus is a masterstroke. It's catchy, jubilant and bold, 'Hark now hear the angels sing ...' It's as if Hairston is shouting from the rooftops, 'Pay attention, folks! This is a big deal!'

Harry Belafonte's version cemented the song's place in Christmas music history, bringing his smooth, reassuring baritone to a song that demands to be sung with both reverence and joy. But it was Boney M's joyously jubilant version that made it an essential on every Christmas party playlist. It's no wonder that 'Mary's Boy Child' endures. It's a reminder that the divine can be both profound and playful, and that sometimes the best way to celebrate is with a bit of a calypso beat.

Video

Merry Xmas Everybody

'MERRY XMAS EVERYBODY' BY SLADE IS THE ROLLICKING, pint-fuelled Yuletide sing-along that crashes through the door of a genteel holiday gathering like a drunken uncle who's come to liven things up. Released in 1973 during the heyday of glam rock, it's a track that eschews the sentimentality and reverence of traditional carols and the schmaltz of the Christmas crooners' catalogue in favour of raucous revelry and unapologetic joy, cranked up loud.

Slade, with their flamboyant outfits and boisterous energy, turned the Christmas season into a no-holds-barred party. From the first guitar riff, 'Merry Xmas Everybody' grabs you by the collar and drags you onto the dance floor. Noddy Holder's raspy opening query about hanging up a stocking sets the tone: this is a song that demands celebration, not contemplation.

The lyrics are a glorious mix of festive nostalgia and rowdy merrymaking. In a cheeky nod to the generational divide, acknowledging the timeless rituals of Christmas while poking fun at their predictability, the song asks if Granny always tells you that 'the old songs are the best'. Then it shifts to the immediate, raucous present: 'Look to the future now ...' It's a call to arms, to embrace the chaos and joy of the season with abandon.

this isn't background music for a quiet evening by the fire, it's the soundtrack to a night of wild, unrestrained festivity

The song was Slade's sixth and final number one and is said by the Performing Rights Society of the United Kingdom to make its writers, Noddy Holder and bassist Jim Lea, £500,000 per year – not bad for a retirement fund. Its popularity shows no signs of abating as every year it can be heard almost everywhere.

Musically, 'Merry Xmas Everybody' is a stomping, infectious romp. With its driving beat, sing-along chorus, and the kind of energy that could power a small village, it's designed to be blasted at full volume. This isn't background music for a quiet evening by the fire; it's the soundtrack to a night of wild, unrestrained festivity. It's a reminder that Christmas can be messy, loud, chaotic, wild and full of genuine, unfiltered merriment.

Video

Rockin' around the Christmas Tree

WRITTEN BY JOHNNY MARKS AND RECORDED BY a 13-year-old Brenda Lee in 1958, 'Rockin' around the Christmas Tree' has become a Christmas classic and a staple of seasonal playlists around the world.

The song captures the joyful spirit of Christmas, with its catchy melody and cheerful lyrics. It tells the story of a festive gathering where friends and family come to celebrate Christmas together. The lyrics evoke a sense of merriment, excitement and nostalgia, conjuring images of an ideal Christmas experience.

With its references to pumpkin pie, carolling, mistletoe and decking the halls with boughs of holly, the whole song is an invitation to everyone to let loose and enjoy the festivities.

The song's popularity can be attributed to its timeless appeal and catchy tune. The melody is instantly recognisable, and the lyrics are easy to sing along to. It has been covered by various artists over the years, each adding their own unique twist to the song while staying true to its joyful spirit.

'Rockin' around the Christmas Tree' has gone on to become a festive classic, cementing its place in popular culture. Most notably, featuring in the much-loved 1990 Christmas movie, *Home Alone*, as Kevin McCallister deters would-be burglars from robbing his home by throwing a pretend Christmas party to make the house appear occupied. It has also been featured in numerous TV shows and commercials.

It has become a seasonal staple of the digital era too, making the song a familiar part of Christmas to audiences of all ages. As if proof of this were needed, in December 2023, sixty-five years after its release, it once again reached number one in the American charts, making Brenda Lee, at the ripe old age of 78, the oldest ever chart topper.

This beloved song embodies the festive spirit of the Christmas season. It has become a holiday classic that continues to bring joy and merriment to people around the world year after year.

Video

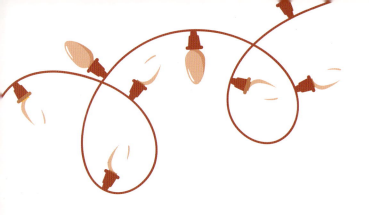

Rudolph the Red-Nosed Reindeer

'RUDOLPH THE RED-NOSED REINDEER' IS THE CHRISTMAS tale of a misfit who turns his unique nasal quirk into a seasonal superpower. Written in 1939 by Robert L. May, the character of Rudolf was at first a marketing ploy for mail-order business Montgomery Ward, and then later immortalised in song by Gene Autry in 1949. This story blends commercialism, whimsy and a touch of circumstantial angst into one of the most beloved holiday legends.

Rudolph starts as the quintessential underdog, ostracised by his peers for his glaringly bright red nose. His fellow reindeer are classic playground bullies, turning their perfectly shaded noses up at anything that deviates from the norm. They laugh, they mock, they exclude. It's a reflection of society's harsh tendency to shun what it doesn't understand. But then, on one foggy Christmas Eve, Santa, the jolly old CEO of the North Pole, realises he's got a logistical nightmare on his hands. Enter Rudolph, whose nasal anomaly becomes the solution to Santa's visibility problem. Suddenly, the reindeer

a sugary coating over a narrative that speaks to anyone who's ever felt like an outsider

who was once the butt of jokes becomes the hero of the night. Rudolph's glowing nose is transformed from a liability into an indispensable asset. The reindeer that nobody wanted to be seen with is now leading the sleigh, guiding the way with his once-mocked beacon. The overnight shift from pariah to hero is as dizzying as it is telling of society's superficiality.

The lyrics make it sound like a neat resolution, 'Then all the reindeer loved him'. Really? After years of exclusion,

Video

111

a single night of utility erases all 'wrongs'? It's a festive Band-Aid over a deeper wound, revealing the fickleness of peer acceptance and the often transactional nature of societal approval.

Musically, 'Rudolph the Red-Nosed Reindeer' is a jaunty, infectious tune, making it a perennial favourite. The jolly melody is in stark contrast to its darker lyrical undertones, a sugary coating over a narrative that speaks to anyone who's ever felt like an outsider. It's a feel-good story about overcoming adversity and finding your place in the world, even if that place is at the front of a sleigh team on a foggy night. So, as you hum along this Christmas, remember that Rudolph's tale is not just about holiday cheer, but also about resilience and the occasional necessity of a glowing nose to guide you through the fog of life.

Santa Claus Is Comin' to Town

'SANTA CLAUS IS COMIN' TO TOWN' IS A POPULAR
Christmas song written by John Frederick Coots and Haven Gillespie. The song was first performed on Eddie Cantor's radio show in November 1934. It was an immediate hit, with orders for over 100,000 copies of sheet music and 30,000 records sold within the first 24 hours of it being performed.

The song's lyrics are simple yet evocative, designed to build excitement and anticipation among children for Santa Claus's arrival on Christmas Eve. It begins with a warning not to pout or cry.

These lines could double as advice from either a life coach or a parole officer, as they set the stage for what is essentially a Christmas compliance checklist. Santa Claus is not just a jolly old man in a red suit; he's a moral auditor with a naughty-or-nice ledger, keeping tabs on your every move. It's the kind of surveillance that would make even George Orwell do a double take.

> Santa Claus is not just a jolly old man in a red suit; he's a moral auditor with a naughty-or-nice ledger, keeping tabs on your every move

But here's the genius: it's all wrapped up in a jaunty, catchy tune that makes the whole idea of an omnipresent, all-seeing Santa who's monitoring everything we do seem like a party. The lyrics assure us that Santa even 'sees you when you're sleeping'. However, this potentially traumatising revelation instead becomes enchanting as it's offset by a playful melody. It's the ultimate carrot-and-stick approach – be good, and you get presents; slip up and, well, who knows.

'Santa Claus Is Comin' to Town' plays into the dual nature of Santa as both a symbol of generosity and a kind of benevolent enforcer. The song manages to be both a delightful celebration of the Christmas spirit and a subtle nudge to keep your behaviour in check – because Santa's list isn't just for show.

Over the years the song has been covered by numerous artists across various genres, solidifying its status as a timeless Christmas classic. Notable versions include those by Bing Crosby, Frank Sinatra, Bruce Springsteen and The Jackson 5. Each of these artists brings their unique style to the song.

The enduring appeal of 'Santa Claus Is Comin' to Town' lies in its sense of fun, festive spirit and the universal excitement it evokes. Whether sung by children eagerly awaiting Santa's visit, or by adults reminiscing about Christmases past, the song remains a quintessential element of the season's soundtrack, and the only one that starts with a warning, 'You better watch out!'

Video

Step into Christmas

'STEP INTO CHRISTMAS' IS ELTON JOHN'S 1973 CONTRIBUTION to the holiday canon, which could best be described as a sugar-fuelled joyride on a sleigh made of sequins, platform boots and synths. This song is like the musical equivalent of a Christmas cardigan: loud, unapologetically festive and likely to cause a few raised eyebrows. It's the kind of track that makes you question if Elton John ever had an off switch, or if he was simply born in a perpetual state of Christmas cheer. It's a full-throttle, sleigh ride through the land of excess and jingle bells. It's as subtle as a snow plough in a shopping centre, and if you're hoping for any kind of nuanced reflection on the season, you won't find it here.

Like all the Elton John hits of the period this was written with lyricist Bernie Taupin. Taupin would send Elton the words and he would make chart-topping hit songs out of them. Right from the opening notes 'Step into Christmas' smacks you in the face with its relentless exuberance. It grabs you by the collar and shakes you like a snow globe. Elton John bursts into the holiday spirit with a piano riff that practically screams, 'Look at me, I'm festive!' It's like he's got a direct line to Santa's workshop and ordered the entire North Pole's worth of glitter and brass for this track. The song is a high-octane dose of Yuletide cheer that's less about sentiment and more about hitting the holiday spirit with a sledgehammer.

Lyrically, the song is about as deep as a puddle on a frosty morning. With lines like 'Step into Christmas ... we can watch the snow fall forever and ever,' you're not exactly diving into deep existential themes. Instead, Elton's busy trying to cram as much holiday spirit into three minutes as possible, leaving you with a tune that's less about reflection and more about sheer, uninhibited festivity.

The production is quintessential 1970s Elton, full of brass, backing vocals, and a pomp that would make a Christmas tree blush. There's no room for subtlety here; it's all about turning the volume up to eleven and seeing if the windows and the neighbours can handle it.

In a world where holiday music often dips into sentimentality and introspection, 'Step into Christmas' is a glorious, glittering exception. It's not about the deeper meanings of the season but about embracing the sheer joy and excess that Christmas can offer – with all the gusto of a Rocket-Man-fuelled holiday bender.

Video

This Christmas

CALLED THE PREMIER CHRISTMAS SONG WRITTEN BY AN African-American, 'This Christmas' is a modern Christmas classic. The song, written and performed by the legendary Donny Hathaway, was first released in 1970. It's soulful and uplifting and has since become a staple in Christmas playlists around the world. With its infectious melody, warm narrative lyrics and Hathaway's always impeccable vocals, 'This Christmas' has stood the test of time and gone on to become one of the 30 most-played Christmas songs in the world, and with each passing year it grows in popularity.

The song opens with a catchy brass riff, accompanied by sleigh bells, setting the festive tone for the rest of the track. Hathaway's smooth and soulful voice then enters, delivering the lyrics with warmth, sincerity and his own unique sonic identity. His vocals effortlessly convey the joy and excitement of the season.

The lyrics of 'This Christmas' celebrate the spirit of togetherness and love that defines Christmas. It's full of Christmas images: hanging the mistletoe, trimming the

Christmas tree, firesides blazing, carolling, presents and cards, etc. Hathaway sings about spending time with loved ones, sharing laughter, joy and memorable moments. He captures the essence of the connections that make Christmas special and reminds us of the importance of nurturing and cherishing our relationships.

Beyond its musical and lyrical brilliance, 'This Christmas' has also had a significant cultural impact. It has been covered by countless artists over the years, including Aretha Franklin, Diana Ross, Seal, Christina Aguilera and many others. It has been featured in numerous movies and television shows, further cementing its status as a Christmas anthem.

'This Christmas' is not just a song; it's a vibe, a feeling that encapsulates the joy and hope of the season in a way that's both contemporary and timeless. It's a reminder that Christmas is as much about the people we spend it with as it is about the traditions we uphold. It brings it back to the basics: good company, good music and the joy of being together.

The song stands out as a unique contribution to the holiday music canon, offering a refreshing take that combines the soul of the seventies with the timeless message of seasonal cheer. It's the perfect soundtrack for a Christmas that's about more than just presents under the tree; it's about the memories we create. It's a song that makes the season brighter, funkier and a whole lot more fun.

Video

119

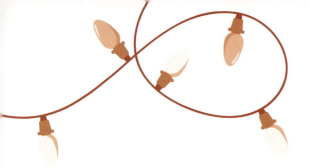

Wonderful Christmastime

'WONDERFUL CHRISTMASTIME' BY PAUL MCCARTNEY IS THE holiday song that epitomises the merry superficiality of the season. Released in 1979, it's the kind of tune that jingles its way into every corner of the holiday season, from crowded shopping centres to office parties, wrapping itself around your brain like a tinsel garrotte.

Picture Sir Paul in his studio, surrounded in all probability by the trappings of late seventies pop opulence, fiddling with his new synthesiser. The result? A song that sounds like it was dashed off between sips of warm cocoa. The song's lyrics are as profound as a cheap Christmas card, 'the spirit's up, we're here tonight'. It's as if McCartney, with all his musical genius, created a mantra for the minimally festive, a reminder that you don't need much to declare it a 'Wonderful Christmastime'.

Video

The melody is catchy in that infuriating way that makes you hum along despite yourself. It's the earworm that you can't shake; the musical equivalent of glitter – you'll be finding traces of it in your life long after the tree is down. McCartney's vocals are light and breezy, and the arrangement feels as dated as an old Polaroid. Yet, like an old Polaroid, it captures something endearing; a snapshot of uncomplicated joy. The song doesn't aim for the heart or the soul; it's content to tickle the ears.

Critics love to hate it, but its staying power is undeniable. 'Wonderful Christmastime' has burrowed into the holiday music canon like a determined squirrel into an attic. Its strength is in its simplicity. This song doesn't aim to evoke deep emotion or profound reflection; it's content with a cheerful nod and a glass of something warm. In a season overloaded with emotional weight and commercial excess, McCartney's ditty offers a respite – a slice of pure, unadulterated Christmas spirit.

In the grand tapestry of Christmas music, 'Wonderful Christmastime' is the equivalent of a plastic reindeer on the lawn – kitsch perhaps, but undeniably part of the tradition. It's not trying to sell you anything profound. It's the soundtrack for trimming the tree, wrapping the presents and pretending you enjoy the office Secret Santa.

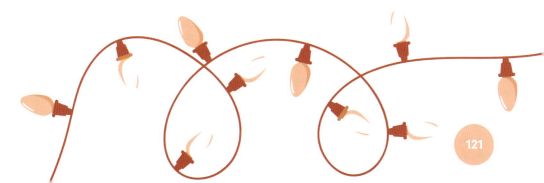

PART
FIVE

Friends & Loved Ones

All I Want for Christmas Is You

'ALL I WANT FOR CHRISTMAS IS YOU' IS A MODERN CLASSIC, first released in 1994 by Mariah Carey, the song has since become one of the most popular Christmas songs of all time. Its catchy melody, cheeky lyrics and Mariah Carey's powerful vocals have made it a perennial Yuletide hit, climbing back up the charts Christmas after Christmas.

From the very first notes in slow free time at the beginning of the song, a joyful and festive tone is set. However, it is the lyrics of 'All I Want for Christmas Is You' that truly resonate with listeners. The song expresses the purest and simplest desire of wanting to be with the person you love at Christmas. It encapsulates the sentiment that material possessions pale in comparison to the joy and happiness that come from being with loved ones. The lyrics convey a genuine longing for connection and emphasise the importance of love and togetherness during Christmas.

Mariah Carey's plaintive vocals bring the lyrics to life, infusing them with emotion and authenticity. Her vocal range and control are showcased throughout the song, and her performance captures the sense of longing and love, making the song relatable and deeply touching for audiences around the world. It should also be mentioned this song is a karaoke favourite over Christmas, with wannabe singers howling their way over the introduction section riffs!

Since its release, 'All I Want for Christmas Is You' has become Mariah Carey's signature song. It has consistently topped the charts and broken records. When it was first released in 1994 it peaked at number six in the United States Adult Contemporary chart and number two in the United Kingdom and Japan. The single broke the record for the longest gap between release and reaching number one, becoming number one in the United States for the first time in 2019 (twenty-five years after release)

a karaoke favourite over Christmas, with wannabe singers howling their way over the introduction section riffs!

and number one for the first time in the United Kingdom in 2020 (twenty-six years after initial release). It has been a December number one in America every year from 2019–2023. It has also become the first Christmas song by a female artist to sell in excess of 10 million copies.

Beyond its commercial success, 'All I Want for Christmas Is You' has also become a symbol of generosity and giving for Mariah Carey. She has used the song's success to support charitable causes, emphasising the importance of reaching out to those most in need during the season of giving.

Video

Baby, It's Cold Outside

'BABY, IT'S COLD OUTSIDE' IS A HOLIDAY SONG THAT'S hotter than a chestnut roasting on an open fire. In equal parts charming and problematic, it's a musical tête-à-tête, a war of words wrapped in wintry charm. Penned by Frank Loesser in 1944, this jazzy, flirtatious duet has become as synonymous with the season as Santa himself, but with a twist that's as spicy as a dash of nutmeg.

Picture this: a cosy living room, a crackling fire and two voices engaged in a game of verbal ping-pong. The man, smooth as bourbon, tries to persuade his lady friend to stay a little longer, while she, equally as suave, plays coy with her excuses. It's a wintertime tango, a battle of wills set to a toe-tapping melody.

However, listening to it with twenty-first-century ears, one can't help but cringe at the undertones of coercion that run through the lyrics. Words like, 'What's in this drink?', take on a more sinister edge in a world more attuned to issues of control and autonomy. Consequently, what was once seen as playful persuasion now reads as something far more problematic. Some see the song as a harmless relic of its time, a playful back-and-forth between two consenting adults. Others argue that its lyrics perpetuate a culture of control and manipulation. Yet, for all its dated dynamics, the song remains a fascinating snapshot of its time. It's a reminder of how far we've come in our understanding of relationships and power balances.

Despite, or perhaps because of, its controversy 'Baby, It's Cold Outside' has endured as a Christmas classic. It's been covered by everyone from Dean Martin to Lady Gaga and Tony Bennett, each bringing their own spin to the age-old dialogue. Some versions lean into the flirtation, while others play up the comedy or dial down the romantic tension. But no matter the interpretation, the song remains a testament to the power of musical storytelling.

In the grand tapestry of holiday music, 'Baby, It's Cold Outside' stands out as a song that's more about the sizzle than the snow. It's a cultural touchstone that forces us to grapple with issues of consent and communication, the ultimate festive flirtation, problematically wrapped up in a frosty bow.

Video

Blue Christmas

'BLUE CHRISTMAS' IS A SONG THAT HAS BECOME associated with the feelings of loneliness, separation and heartache that many experience during the Christmas season. The song was penned by Billy Hayes and Jay W. Johnson in 1948, and its mournful melody was eventually immortalised by Elvis Presley in 1957, turning a simple country ballad into an anthem for the lovelorn.

The song's charm lies in its brutal honesty. The sadness of a 'blue Christmas without you', is not just a line, but a gut punch to anyone who's ever felt the sting of loneliness while everyone else is busy decking halls, hanging mistletoe and planning get-togethers. Elvis's rendition, with his deep, velvety voice dripping with Southern sorrow, elevated the song from mere melancholy to a cathartic experience. It went to number one on the 1957 Billboard Christmas chart and was the most popular song from Elvis's Christmas

Album, the top-selling Christmas album of all time with sales well in excess of 20 million.

The song paints a picture of someone feeling alone and bereft, surrounded by the festive cheer that only serves to heighten their sense of loss. It captures the conflicting emotions that many feel at Christmas, of wanting to be happy and joyful but being unable to escape feelings of emptiness and heartbreak.

Despite its sombre theme, 'Blue Christmas' continues to be a staple on Christmas playlists, reminding us that Christmas is not always a joyous time for everyone. It serves as a reminder of the importance of empathy and compassion, encouraging us to reach out to those who may be feeling isolated or alone. Beyond its emotional impact, 'Blue Christmas' has also become a symbol of nostalgia and a reflection of the changing times. It captures a sentiment that transcends generations, reminding us that even in moments of sadness, we can find solace in shared experiences.

'Blue Christmas' stands as a testament to the power of music to connect and console, providing solace to those who find themselves longing for loved ones at Christmas. It's the song that says, 'If this time of year is hard for you, you're not alone, you're seen and you're understood.'

Video

Christmas (Baby Please Come Home)

'CHRISTMAS (BABY PLEASE COME HOME)' IS THE SONG that single-handedly puts the raw emotion back into the holiday season, yanking you out of the holly-jolly haze and right into the heartache of unwrapped loneliness. Written by the powerhouse trio of Phil Spector, Jeff Barry and Ellie Greenwich, and sung by Darlene Love (of *20 Feet from Stardom* fame), this 1963 classic is the musical equivalent of a neon sign flashing 'SADNESS INSIDE' over a festive backdrop.

The song starts with a cascade of Spector's 'Wall of Sound', an orchestral avalanche that swallows you whole before Darlene even gets a word in. When she does, it's with a voice that could move mountains. However, as she opens, singing about the snow coming down, instead of a picturesque winter wonderland, it feels like the universe conspiring to highlight her solitude. This is the song for the one staring at the door, hoping for a miracle, a high-octane plea wrapped in a festive disguise. It's about missing someone so much it hurts, especially when surrounded by a world obsessed with joy and togetherness. It's the soundtrack for those who find Christmas hard without their loved ones.

Darlene Love's powerhouse vocals are the heart and soul of this track. She belts out the lyrics with a kind of raw, unfiltered emotion that makes you believe she really is sitting alone by the Christmas tree, pining for a lost love. It's the sound of holiday desperation, turned up to eleven. And then there's Phil Spector's production, a symphonic cacophony of bells, strings and background vocals that hits you like a tinsel-covered battering ram.

Over the decades, this song has seen numerous covers. U2 gave it a rock twist, Mariah Carey turned it into a vocal showcase and Michael Bublé smoothed it out for the crooner crowd. Yet, no matter who sings it, the core remains unshaken – an unfiltered expression of longing and hope that resonates with anyone who's ever spent Christmas alone, waiting. In the pantheon of holiday music, 'Christmas (Baby Please Come Home)' stands out as the anthem of the disenchanted. It's a stark reminder that behind the festive facade, Christmas can be a time of deep yearning.

Video

Fairytale of New York

IN THE REALM OF ROCK AND ROLL, THERE ARE SONGS that transcend time and become anthems for generations. One such anthem is 'Fairytale of New York', a heartfelt and bittersweet ballad by The Pogues, featuring Kirsty MacColl. Released in 1987, this iconic track has since become a staple of holiday playlists, capturing the essence of both Christmas cheer and the gritty realities of life in the Big Apple.

The Pogues, led by Shane MacGowan, weave a tale of love, loss and redemption against the backdrop of New York City. MacGowan's gravelly vocals bring the characters to life as he portrays a troubled and disillusioned Irish immigrant. His interplay with Kirsty MacColl is nothing short of magical, their voices intertwining in a perfect symmetry that encapsulates the raw emotions of the narrative. The lyrics paint a vivid picture of a couple whose dreams have been shattered by addiction, despair and disappointment.

133

Opening with a line that sets the scene on Christmas Eve in a 'drunk tank' we are immediately introduced to a tale that is equal parts melancholic and hopeful. The verses are filled with poetic imagery, describing the neon lights of Times Square, the snow-covered streets, and the bitter cold that permeates the city. As the song progresses, we are taken on a journey of love and disappointment, as the couple reminisce about their past and grapple with the harsh reality of their present. The lyrics are filled with raw emotion and biting wit, capturing the complex dynamics of a relationship on the brink.

Musically, 'Fairytale of New York' is a masterclass in arrangement. The Pogues' signature blend of traditional Irish instruments, including the tin whistle and accordion, is interwoven with a driving rhythm section. The result is a dynamic sound that perfectly complements the emotional depth of the lyrics. The song reaches its climax with the iconic chorus with a quick dash of sentiment, as the NYPD choir sing 'Galway Bay' and the Christmas bells ring. The vocal melody in the chorus is in two parts, separate and then together, creating a beautiful and unusual merging of the tune.

This gritty tale of the marginalised, full of dark humour, has become a modern classic and an essential part of the Christmas canon. It is a fairytale like no other, a love letter both to the Christmas season and to New York City, and a song that will continue to enchant audiences for generations.

Video

Feliz Navidad

MERRY CHRISTMAS, 'FELIZ NAVIDAD' IN SPANISH: THE VERY phrase carries a sense of warmth, joy and celebration. Let us paint a picture of the act of 'doing Feliz Navidad'. Imagine a bustling town square, adorned with twinkling lights and vibrant decorations. Families and friends gather, filled with excitement and anticipation. As the clock strikes midnight, signalling the arrival of Christmas Day, a chorus of voices rises in unison, singing the familiar words of 'Feliz Navidad'. People of all ages join in, creating a symphony of goodwill and togetherness. The song becomes a symbol of unity. It is a moment of shared happiness, where the barriers that separate us crumble, and we are reminded of our common humanity. But the song that has become the soundtrack to all this, was almost never written.

In 1970, Puerto Rican superstar José Feliciano was recording an album of Christmas songs when his producer suggested that he write a new song for the album. Feliciano thought it impractical in the time available, but then reminisced about his childhood in Puerto Rico and the Christmases of his youth, and soon 'Feliz Navidad' was born. It's now been covered internationally by hundreds of artists, becoming a traditional part of the Christmas-time musical landscape, and is one of the top twenty-five most played and recorded Christmas songs around the world.

In this song, José Feliciano was writing about the essence of 'doing Feliz Navidad', which goes beyond just singing a song. It involves embracing the spirit of giving and spreading love. It involves reaching out to others, extending a helping hand and making a difference in someone's life. It involves acts of kindness and generosity, big or small, that have the power to brighten someone's day.

In the spirit of 'Feliz Navidad', families come together to prepare traditional foods, they gather around the table, their hearts and stomachs full, cherishing the company of loved ones. They exchange gifts, not merely as material possessions, but as symbols of love and appreciation. As the night draws in, the echoes of 'Feliz Navidad' linger in the air, a reminder of the joy and unity that Christmas can bring. It is a celebration that reminds us of the power of love and the beauty of the human spirit. And this song, 'Feliz Navidad', has become one of its modern anthems.

Video

Last Christmas

'LAST CHRISTMAS' IS A MODERN CLASSIC THAT HAS NEVER waned in popularity since its release in 1984. Written by George Michael and performed by Wham!, this bittersweet ballad of doomed romance, has become a Christmas staple, capturing the essence of both love and heartbreak during Christmas time. George Michael croons about wounds that are fresh enough to sting but seasoned with just enough nostalgia to make you think, 'Ah, the good old days — if only they weren't so awful.'

The song kicks off with the perfect juxtaposition of festive generosity ('I gave you my heart') and emotional betrayal ('you gave it away'), all wrapped up in a catchy pop melody. The song's beauty lies in its simplicity; it's a lament of love lost, but not too lost, since it's re-lived annually. The song was recorded in the height of summer and was practically a DIY production, with every instrument played by George Michael.

What makes 'Last Christmas' enduring is its blend of synth-driven melodies and its all-too-relatable narrative of misplaced trust and romantic disillusionment. George Michael sings with the knowingness of someone who's been wronged but is just self-aware enough to acknowledge the melodrama of it all. The song's upbeat tempo belies its melancholic undercurrent, making it the perfect soundtrack for wrapping gifts and pondering life's little ironies.

the song's upbeat tempo belies its melancholic undercurrent

And then there's the iconic music video: a snow-covered Alpine retreat filled with oversized sweaters, feathered and back-combed hair, and meaningful glances over hot cocoa. It's a visual time capsule of eighties fashion and aesthetic, making people nostalgic for a time many of them never actually lived through.

Beyond its musical and visual impact, 'Last Christmas' is a symbol of generosity and giving. On its initial release in 1984 the song spent five weeks at number two in the United Kingdom as, 'Do They Know It's Christmas?', the famine relief record by Band Aid, was number one. Wham!, who were also featured on the Band Aid record, donated all their royalties from 'Last Christmas' to Ethiopian famine relief.

Since around 2010, 'Last Christmas' has been the subject of the increasingly popular game of 'Whamageddon'. Players attempt to go from 1 December to the end of Christmas Eve without hearing 'Last Christmas'. Any player hearing the song between those dates is out, and has to post '#Whamageddon' on social media to show they've lost the challenge.

With all of this said, perhaps its most profound resonance has come since the tragic death of George Michael on Christmas Day in 2016. Since then, 'Last Christmas' has achieved something it never managed during George's lifetime. It reached number one in the UK singles chart for the first time in 2023, thirty-nine years and over 4 million sales after its initial release. And in December 2024 it became the first song to be the UK's Christmas number one in two consecutive years.

'Last Christmas' by Wham! is a testament to the enduring power of Christmas music. It encapsulates the joy, heartbreak, hope and regret that can be experienced at Christmas.

Video

139

Lonely This Christmas

'LONELY THIS CHRISTMAS' BY MUD IS THE KIND OF song that makes you wonder if the Brits are genetically incapable of doing Christmas without a healthy dose of misery. Released in 1974 when it was that year's Christmas chart topper, this little gem of festive cheer is essentially Elvis Presley's 'Blue Christmas' reimagined by people who thought that song wasn't depressing enough, so they ramped up the heartbreak, threw in some bitter resentment, and, voilà – a festive anthem.

The song was written by Nicky Chinn and Mike Chapman who were serial hit makers in the 1970s, creating a string of hits for The Sweet, Suzi Quatro, Mud and Racey. Between the beginning of 1973 and the end of 1974 they had nineteen UK Top 40 hits, including five number ones. 'Lonely This Christmas' is, as the title suggests, all about loneliness. Not just the everyday kind, but that special brand of

loneliness reserved for 25 December – the one time of year when, for some, being alone feels like a personal failure. Mud unerringly managed to capture that festive despair with an Elvis impersonation so uncanny it makes you question whether the King might have sneaked over to the UK just to make a few extra quid from a Christmas single.

Musically, it's dripping with slow, weepy guitar riffs and aching vocals. The lyrics wallow in misery. It's all about how his love is gone, and he's left sitting by the tree, alone, probably with a bottle of mulled wine and a turkey dinner for one.

Most Christmas songs at least try to bring some kind of cheer, but not this one. This one's happy to sit with you in the darkness, staring out the window at other people's happiness like some masochistic holiday voyeur. This was highlighted by the band's Christmas performance on *Top of the Pops*. Lead singer, Les Gray, illustrated his isolation by singing the entire song to a ventriloquist's dummy!

In short, 'Lonely This Christmas' is what happens when you take all the joy out of the season and replace it with a big heap of melancholy. For those who find it helpful to lean into the loneliness they feel at Christmas, this is the song for you.

Video

141

Stay Another Day

'STAY ANOTHER DAY' BY EAST 17 IS THE CHRISTMAS SONG
that crashed the holiday party like an uninvited guest and
somehow ended up being the life and soul of it. Released
in 1994, this ballad with its plush strings and sleigh bells
somehow sneaked into the festive playlist, elbowing aside
the usual cheer for a dose of grief, loss and raw emotion
wrapped in a big boy-band bow.

It was the mid-1990s, boy bands were brooding and East 17,
the bad boys of British pop, dropped this tear-jerker that
muscled its way into the Christmas canon. ony Mortimer, the
band's main songwriter, penned it after his brother tragically
took his own life, a detail that casts a shadow over the song's
otherwise shimmering pop production.

The lyrics are a plea, a last-ditch effort to keep a life and
a loved one from slipping away, 'we've come too far now

... to throw it all away', sing the band, making you think less of mistletoe and more of missed opportunities. It's a potent emotional message that leaves you teetering between nostalgia and outright despair. The song begs for another day, another chance, wrapped in a melody that's as sticky as a Christmas pudding. The song was never meant to be a Christmas song, but the sleigh bells were added and the promo video featuring the band in their white fur parkas confirmed its status as a Christmas classic.

Despite its sombre undertones, 'Stay Another Day' soared to the top of the UK charts. Tony Mortimer tells the story of the royalty cheque for the song arriving in the post and his disbelief at how many zeroes were on the end of the amount.

The song's success lies in its ability to tap into the bittersweet nature of the season – the mix of joy and sorrow, of beginnings and endings. It's the Christmas song for the ones nursing broken hearts amidst the tinsel and twinkling lights, a reminder that the festive season for many of us isn't just about cheer, but also about facing the cold realities of life and loss.

Video

143

The Twelve Days of Christmas

'THE TWELVE DAYS OF CHRISTMAS' IS A POPULAR SONG that tells the story of 364 gifts given over the course of twelve days. The days in question are the old traditional twelve days of Christmas, lasting from Christmas Day to the end of 5 January (Twelfth Night), the day before Epiphany, which is sometimes also called Three Kings Day.

The earliest known publication of the words to 'The Twelve Days of Christmas' were in an illustrated children's book, *Mirth Without Mischief*, published in London in 1780. However, the origins may go back as far as the early 1600s, making it probably the oldest non-religious Christmas song still regularly sung today. It is one of the most popular

Christmas songs in the world. Over the centuries, a number of different melodies have been associated with the song. The one we sing today is from a 1909 arrangement by English composer Frederic Austin.

Although the song has gone through numerous lyrical variations over time, it has returned to being identical to the 1780 version, with one exception. The original first line was, 'On the first day of Christmas my true love sent to me', today has been changed to, 'gave to me'. It then continues with a new gift being added each day. The gifts mentioned in the song are varied and unusual, ranging from birds to musicians, to dancers, to milkmaids. The gifts have been interpreted in different ways over the years. Some believe them to represent Christian religious symbols, while others see them as simply an inventory of increasingly more extravagant presents.

> the highlight of the song is the grand singing of, 'Five Gold Rings', followed by an ever-accelerating rendition of the remainder of the list

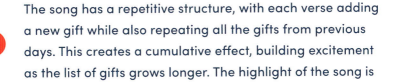

The song has a repetitive structure, with each verse adding a new gift while also repeating all the gifts from previous days. This creates a cumulative effect, building excitement as the list of gifts grows longer. The highlight of the song is the grand singing of, 'Five Gold Rings', followed by an ever-accelerating rendition of the remainder of the list.

'The Twelve Days of Christmas' has been adapted and reimagined in various forms, including books, movies and stage productions. It has also been parodied and humorously modified in popular culture. It is often performed in schools, churches and community gatherings during the Christmas season. In addition to its musical appeal, the song also carries a message of generosity and gift-giving, reflecting in a humorous way both the spirit of Christmas largesse or, depending on your viewpoint, excess.

Video

We Wish You a Merry Christmas

'WE WISH YOU A MERRY CHRISTMAS' IS A CHEERFUL and popular Christmas carol with a catchy melody and memorable festive lyrics that's been a seasonal favourite for centuries.

Its origins can be traced back to sixteenth-century England. It is believed to have originated as a traditional English folk song, sung by carollers as they went from door to door, spreading Christmas cheer and good wishes. The song's repetitive and joyful nature reflects the spirit of celebration and togetherness during the Christmas season. Its lyrics carry a simple and heartfelt message, conveying warm wishes for a merry Christmas and a happy New Year. While many Christmas carols are based on the biblical story of Christmas and carry a religious message, 'We wish you a Merry Christmas' is a sing-along exception.

One interesting aspect of the song is its mention of 'figgy pudding' in the second verse. Figgy pudding is the precursor to Christmas pudding in the UK and plum pudding in the USA. The mention of this traditional treat adds a touch of culinary delight to the song and reflects the customs and traditions associated with bygone Christmases in Britain where carollers sang door to door

a traditional English folk song, sung by carollers as they went from door to door

and were usually rewarded with a treat of some sort. In fact, there are numerous tales of carollers only stopping their singing when the occupants of the house they were singing outside gave them money, a gift or food. Hence the 'figgy pudding' line being followed by 'And we won't go until we've got some'.

Over the years, 'We Wish You a Merry Christmas' has been embraced by people of various cultures and has been translated into numerous languages. The song's popularity has led to countless renditions and adaptations by artists and musicians worldwide. It has been recorded in various musical styles, from classical to pop, and has been featured in movies, commercials and Christmas-themed events.

Beyond its musical appeal, 'We Wish You a Merry Christmas' encapsulates the essence of the season. It serves as a link between Christmas past and Christmas present and is a reminder to cherish the company of loved ones, to spread joy and goodwill, to express gratitude for the blessings of the year gone by and to wholeheartedly embrace the possibilities of the year ahead.

Video

PART SIX

Songs
for the
World

Do They Know It's Christmas?

'DO THEY KNOW IT'S CHRISTMAS?' BECAME EMBLEMATIC of the celebrity-driven charity records of the 1980s. Written by Bob Geldof and Midge Ure, the track was recorded in 1984 by an ensemble of predominantly British and Irish musicians (joined by Shalamar and Kool & the Gang) under the name Band Aid. Its purpose was to raise awareness and funds for the famine-stricken population of Ethiopia. The song quickly became a massive hit, topping charts and spurring similar humanitarian efforts.

Musically, 'Do They Know It's Christmas?' is a quintessential eighties' pop song, characterised by its synthesisers, grand production and a catchy chorus. It begins with a solemn,

low-key tone but quickly shifts to a more uplifting and anthemic sound, fitting its message of hope and collective action. The chorus is both memorable and repetitive, ensuring its place in the listener's mind long after the song has ended.

The song's lyrics were problematic for some; they ask if the starving Ethiopians even know it's Christmas. One might respond, 'Yes, they do, as Ethiopia was one of the first cradles of Christianity', but the song itself wasn't about the Ethiopians. It was about making Western audiences feel like they were able to do something positive, to make a difference from the relative comfort of their own lives.

Bob Geldof and Midge Ure opened their little black books and assembled a stellar line-up, a veritable who's who of eighties' pop, from Bono to Boy George, taking in Sting, Phil Collins, U2, Duran Duran and a cast of pop royalty, all assembled to deliver lines that ranged from the awkwardly naive to the downright patronising. Bono croons an uncomfortable line, encouraging us to thank God that it isn't us this time! Nothing says Christmas spirit like a good old dose of survivor's guilt.

it sold in excess of 12 million copies and has raised over £25 million for famine relief

Despite these criticisms, 'Do They Know It's Christmas?' succeeded in its primary goal: it sold in excess of 12 million

copies and has raised over £25 million for famine relief. In doing so it ensured that the need for action stayed at the forefront of the news cycle and the collective consciousness. It established a blueprint for celebrity activism, setting a precedent for future charity singles, including USA for Africa's 'We Are the World', and was the forerunner to the Live Aid concert in 1985, which many consider a defining moment of the decade.

'Do They Know It's Christmas?' remains a staple of holiday playlists, but the song's lasting legacy is as a testament to the power of music to mobilise resources and attention for humanitarian causes, which surely chimes loudly with the spirit of Christmas.

Video

Go Tell It on the Mountain

'GO TELL IT ON THE MOUNTAIN' ISN'T JUST A CHRISTMAS carol; it's a spiritual firecracker! Forget your jingling bells and roasting chestnuts – this Christmas carol barrels into the room like a revival preacher with a megaphone, demanding your undivided attention. The song is rooted in African-American spirituals, a genre that marries deep-seated pain with transcendent hope. It was popularised by the Fisk Jubilee Singers, the first internationally renowned Black spiritual ensemble. 'Go Tell It on the Mountain' is less about subtle holiday cheer and more about shouting the good news from every rooftop.

The opening line, 'Go tell it on the mountain, over the hills and everywhere', is more than just an invitation, it's a demand. There's no room for ambiguity here; the message is clear and unyielding: Christ is born, and you'd better tell the world about it.

Picture it: the nineteenth century, a time when spirituals were the clandestine lifeblood of a community bound in chains, 'Go Tell It on the Mountain' emerged from this crucible as an anthem of liberation disguised as a hymn. It wasn't about decking the halls; it was about proclaiming freedom and divine justice from every hill and dale.

John Wesley Work Jr brought this song into the public eye in 1907, but it had already been echoing in the hearts and voices of the oppressed for decades. The lyrics are a straightforward, no-nonsense call to action, 'Go tell it on the mountain, over the hills and everywhere'. You can almost hear the urgency, the burning need to spread the good news like a wildfire.

This isn't a carol for the faint of heart. It's been belted out by everyone from Mahalia Jackson, who infused it with gospel fervour, to Bruce Springsteen, who gave it a gritty, working-man's edge. Each rendition transforms it, yet the core message remains as unshakeable as a mountain: Christ is born, and that's news worth shouting about.

'Go Tell It on the Mountain' is a refreshing jolt to the often saccharine Christmas playlist. It's a reminder that some stories are so good that they need to be shouted from the rooftops, or in this case, the mountaintops. It's a celebration of radical joy, a defiant proclamation of hope that dares to echo from the highest peaks.

Video

Good King Wenceslas

'GOOD KING WENCESLAS' IS THE CHRISTMAS CAROL that makes you wonder if the holiday spirit ever took a detour through a medieval audit. Written by John Mason Neale in 1853, this carol presents Christmas as less of a cosy, twinkling affair and more of a rigorous exercise in charitable bureaucracy. If Santa Claus is the embodiment of holiday jolliness, then King Wenceslas is the stern-faced civil servant ensuring that everyone's Christmas compliance is up to scratch. The 'Feast of Stephen' referenced in the carol is 26 December. Many medieval churches would have alms boxes for distributing food and gifts to the poor on that day. Hence it became known as Boxing Day and synonymous with Christmas giving.

This carol tells the tale of the historical Bohemian King Wenceslas, who rather than sitting comfortably on his throne, decides to brave a snowstorm to deliver food and drink to a poor peasant in person. It's a nice touch really, nothing says 'season of goodwill' like a monarch engaged in hands-on charity work. The story might be charming if it weren't for the fact that Wenceslas's idea of a good time involves trudging through the snow, dealing with frostbite and carrying sacks of provisions like he's auditioning for 'Survivor: Medieval Edition'.

Musically, 'Good King Wenceslas' is upbeat and brisk, with a melody that's as straightforward as the king's intentions. It's the kind of tune that could be played by a brass band, while a group of actors in fur-lined capes re-enact Wenceslas's snowy journey. The line, 'Bring me flesh and bring me wine', is less about culinary delights and more about driving home the point that charity is all about action.

What's especially delightful about this carol is its practical spirit. While most Christmas songs focus on the ethereal and the festive, 'Good King Wenceslas' gets down to the bare bones of holiday responsibility. What's delightful about 'Good King Wenceslas' is its no-nonsense approach to Christmas. While other carols might focus on the birth of Jesus or the joys of the season, 'Good King Wenceslas' is out there trudging through the snow, ensuring that charity remains a central part of Christmas. It's a royal reminder that sometimes, the true spirit of Christmas is about rolling up your sleeves and getting a little bit cold and wet for the sake of others.

Video

Happy Xmas (War Is Over)

'HAPPY XMAS (WAR IS OVER)' IS JOHN LENNON AND YOKO Ono's earnest plea for the gift of peace at Christmas. Released in 1971, it's a song that's more a political manifesto set to music than a simple holiday tune. It's a clarion call to wake up from our seasonal consumerist stupor and actually care about the world. Lennon wasn't interested in presents or family dinners, he wanted to stir our consciences, to ask the hard questions, and in true Lennon fashion, it carries all the subtlety of a brick through a window.

The opening chords ring out with a sombre optimism, and you can almost hear Lennon's world-weary sigh in every note. He's asking us to reflect, to look in the mirror and ponder the state of humanity. His lyric starkly asks us, What have you done?' It's a question that lands with weight. For Lennon, it wasn't enough to string up some lights. He wanted action, he wanted change and he wanted it now.

The vocals are unpolished, out of tune in places, giving the song a sense of urgent gravitas, telling the listener that the message is more important than the performance.

Yoko's presence, meanwhile, adds a haunting echo to Lennon's gravelly sincerity. Together, they conjure an atmosphere that's more about silent nights of contemplation than jingling bells and Santa's, 'Ho-ho-ho'. The children's choir joins in, tugging at your heartstrings with their innocent voices, making it clear that this isn't just about us – it's about the future we're leaving them.

Yet, for all its earnestness, 'Happy Xmas (War Is Over)' can sometimes feel like a case of preaching to the choir. It's a song beloved by those already inclined to agree with its message. The people who need to hear it the most are probably too busy shopping to listen.

Lennon's utopian vision clashes head-on with the reality of Christmas in a capitalist society. It's as if he's reminding us that while we're busy wrapping presents, we might want to wrap our heads around the notion of peace on earth.

This song has a staying power that can't be denied. It captures John and Yoko's genuine belief in the power of music to change the world, an idea and ideal that many still cling too today. So, this Christmas, give a nod to John Lennon and Yoko Ono. Their dream of a peaceful world may still seem a distant hope, but at least they had the courage to dream it.

Video

The Little Drummer Boy

'THE LITTLE DRUMMER BOY' HAS CAPTURED THE HEARTS of millions around the world. Written by Katherine Kennicott Davis in 1941, this timeless carol tells the story of a young boy who, despite having no gift to bring, offers his musical talent as a humble tribute to the baby Jesus.

The song opens with the line, 'Come, they told me', followed by the tune's iconic 'pa rum pum pum pum'. The simple words instantly transport us to the scene of the nativity, where the boy is summoned to witness the birth of Jesus. The repetitive and rhythmic nature of the lyrics mimics the beat of the drummer boy's drum and, as the song progresses, we learn about the drummer boy's internal conflict. He yearns

to honour the newborn King but feels inadequate because he lacks a material gift to bring unlike the other visitors. However, he soon realises that he can offer something unique and meaningful – his drumming skills. With a tender heart and unwavering determination, he plays his drum for the baby Jesus, creating a beautiful and heartfelt rhythm.

'The Little Drummer Boy' carries a powerful message about the true spirit of Christmas. It reminds us that it is not the grandness or material value of our gifts that matter, but the sincerity and love with which they are offered. The song emphasises that each person has something that is special to offer, regardless of their circumstances or possessions.

The lyrics depict the drummer boy's encounter with Jesus as a transformative and deeply personal experience. As he plays his drum, he sees that his humble offering touches the heart of the newborn King, he experiences a sense of acceptance and belonging, despite his lack of material wealth. This profound encounter speaks of the value of sincerity of heart above all else.

Beyond its musical qualities, the lyrics of 'The Little Drummer Boy' remind us that Christmas is a time of giving, not just of material possessions, but in the offering of our talents, love and compassion. As we listen to and sing the song, we are reminded of the powerful message it carries. It inspires us to remember that the greatest gift we can offer is the genuine expression of our love and devotion. It also reminds us of the power of simplicity, the beauty of selfless giving and the significance of the humblest of offerings.

Video

Peace on Earth/Little Drummer Boy

FROM THE TRADITIONAL 'LITTLE DRUMMER BOY' CAME
'Peace on Earth/Little Drummer Boy'. This peculiar duet
between David Bowie and Bing Crosby from 1977 is a
bizarre cultural artefact, blending the avant-garde with the
traditional in a way that's both baffling and beguiling. The
song pairs the classic 'Little Drummer Boy' from 1941 with
'Peace on Earth', an original piece written for the 1977 duet.
The result is a song that feels like a cultural bridge between
two very different eras.

Imagine the setup: Bing Crosby, the embodiment of old-school, cardigan-clad Christmas cheer, invites David Bowie, the alien rock god known for his androgynous glam and space-age oddities, onto his holiday special. The resulting duet is a surreal collision of worlds. Crosby, with his smooth, timeless croon and Bowie, with his ethereal voice and edgy persona, should have been an oil-and-water mix. Instead, they produced a harmonious blend that somehow made sense in the fractured reality of the late seventies.

the contrast between Bing Crosby's old-school crooning and Bowie's contemporary flair shouldn't work, but it does – beautifully

Musically, the song abuts the solemn 'Little Drummer Boy' with the newly penned 'Peace on Earth', creating a dialogue between the old and the new, the sacred and the contemporary. Bowie's 'Peace on Earth' overlays Crosby's 'Little Drummer Boy' with an earnest plea for global harmony, a sentiment that seems desperately needed today. The arrangement is lush and understated, letting the vocals shine in their strange symbiosis.

Lyrically, it's an intriguing juxtaposition. 'Little Drummer Boy' sticks to its simple, hypnotic, 'pa-rum-pum-pum-pum', while 'Peace on Earth' offers a heartfelt call for awareness and compassion, 'Every child must be made to care'. It's as

if Bowie is gently nudging Crosby's nostalgic reverie into the contemporary world, reminding us that while we're indulging in holiday traditions, there's a bigger picture that needs our attention.

In the pantheon of Christmas music 'Peace on Earth/Little Drummer Boy' is a delightful anomaly. It captures a unique moment in time, when two vastly different artists came together to create something unexpected. The contrast between Bing Crosby's old-school crooning and Bowie's contemporary flair shouldn't work, but it does – beautifully. It's a heady mix of the traditional and the modern, the sacred and the secular, wrapped up in a package that somehow makes sense. The song became an instant classic, not just for its unusual pairing but for its message – a timely reminder that Christmas is about more than just presents and pageantry; it's about peace, goodwill and the little things we can all contribute.

Video

Mistletoe and Wine

'MISTLETOE AND WINE' BY CLIFF RICHARD IS THE EPITOME of eighties' Christmas pop: unashamedly earnest, festooned with festive clichés, and as warm and fuzzy as a reindeer sweater. Released in 1988, this song is like a holiday fruitcake – rich, dense and filled with traditional ingredients. It's warm, cosy and unabashedly festive, like a Yuletide manifesto celebrating all things Christmas with gusto.

The lyrics read like a shopping list for an ideal Christmas, 'a time for giving', 'a time for believing' rounded off with children singing and logs on the fire. It's the kind of song that makes you feel like you're starring in your own Christmas special, complete with slow-motion hugs and twinkling lights. Cliff belts out lines about peace on earth with the conviction of a man who has yet to encounter a Black Friday sale.

The song was written by Jeremy Paul, Leslie Stewart and Keith Strachan for a musical adaptation of Hans Christian Andersen's *The Little Match Girl*. It was written as an ironic ditty to be sung as the little match girl was thrown outside into the cold. Cliff Richard liked the song but sought the writers' permission to change some of the lyrics to adopt a more Christian theme. Although only released in late November, it became the biggest selling single of the year, the Christmas number one of 1988 and the third best-selling single of the entire decade. In fact, Cliff has had quite the run of Christmas chart toppers, five to date, including three in a row, 1988 – 'Mistletoe and Wine', 1989 – 'Do They Know It's Christmas?' (Band Aid 2) and 1990 – 'Saviour's Day'.

the kind of song that makes you feel like you're starring in your own Christmas special

The charm, or perhaps the kitsch, of 'Mistletoe and Wine' lies in its utter lack of irony. There's no tongue-in-cheek, no post-modern wink; it's all straight-faced sentiment. Cliff Richard delivers his message with such sincerity that you almost forget how many times you've heard it before. It's a song about peace and goodwill sung with the sincerity of a man who truly believes every word. It's a song that wears its heart on its sleeve.

Video

When a Child Is Born

'WHEN A CHILD IS BORN' IS A SONG THAT TAPS INTO A universal sense of wonder and renewal with its hopeful and uplifting lyrics. Released in 1974, it's become a staple of the holiday season, praised for its powerful message of peace and the transformative power of new life. Its lyrics, coupled with its sweeping melody, create a feeling of reverence and joy that resonates deeply with listeners. The melody began life in 1970 in a song called, 'Tränen lügen nicht', ('Tears Do Not Lie') by Michael Holm, eventually transforming into the score published by Fred Jacobson and Ciro Dammicco. The English Christmas song lyrics were put to the melody later by Austrian composer Fred Jay.

The song begins with the evocative image of 'a ray of hope' flickering in the sky, setting the tone for a narrative about the birth of a child bringing profound change. With imagery such as 'a brand new dawn' appearing across the land, the lyrics suggest the Christmas story, while maintaining a certain ambiguity by never directly mentioning shepherds, angels, wise men or the birth of Jesus. Instead, they declare that the arrival of a new baby is not just a personal milestone but a beacon of optimism for the world.

Musically, 'When a Child Is Born' is characterised by its orchestral arrangement and poignant melody, which enhance the song's emotional impact. The lush arrangement, and in the case of the 1976 Johnny Mathis version, impeccable vocal delivery, amplify the song's themes of hope and transformation. Lyrics such as 'a silent wish' sailing 'the seven seas' evoke a sense of global unity and aspiration, reflecting the song's broader message of collective hope and peace.

Despite its idealistic portrayal, the song's strength lies in its ability to evoke genuine feelings of warmth and optimism. It celebrates the profound impact that new life has on individuals and the world, capturing a sentiment that is both deeply personal and universally resonant. Is it a religious or a secular Christmas song? Is it about new birth in general or a specific birth? This very cleverly penned song is whatever the listener chooses it to be. In essence, 'When a Child Is Born' is a touching reminder of the potential for positive change that new life brings, making it a timeless piece for Christmas and beyond.

Video

Index

Credits

All I Want for Christmas Is You

Carey, M., Afanasieff, W. (1994). Beyondidolization and Universal Music, both administered by Universal Music Publishing Group; Sony/ATV Tunes Inc. and Tavla Vista Music, both administered by Sony Music Publishing; and Hipgnosis SFH I Ltd, administered by Kobalt.

Angels from the Realms of Glory

Montgomery, J. (1816) Public Domain.

Away in a Manger

Spilman, J. (1837). Public Domain.

Baby, It's Cold Outside

Loesser, F. (1944). Frank Music Corp.

Blue Christmas

Hayes, B., Johnson, J. W. (1948). Demi Music Corp d.b.a Lichelle Music Co/Demi Music Corp dba Lichelle Music/ Universal-MCA Music Publishing/Universal- Polygram/ Universal-Polygram International Publishing.

Carol of the Bells

Leontovich, M. (1919). Carl Fischer, LLC.

Christmas (Baby Please Come Home)

Barry, J., Greenwich, A., Spector, P. (1963). Universal – Songs of Polygram International Inc. Abkco Music Inc. Trio Music Company, Inc. and EMI Blackwood Music Inc. o.b.o. Mother Bertha Music, Inc.

Coventry Carol

Traditional. Public Domain.

Deck the Halls

Traditional. Public Domain.

Ding Dong Merrily on High

Traditional / Woodward, G. R. (1924). Public domain.

Do They Know It's Christmas?

Geldof, B., Ure, M. (1984). Chappell Music Ltd.

Do You Hear What I Hear?

Regney, N., Shayne, G. (1962). Jewel Music Publishing Co Inc.

Fairytale of New York

MacGowan, S., Finer, J. (1987). Downtown Copyright Mgmt d.b.a Dtcm Blvd o.b.o. Spz Music Inc and Universal – Polygram International Pub Inc. o.b.o. Universal Music Publishing Limited.

Feliz Navidad

Feliciano, J. (1914). BMG Gold Songs o.b.o J&H Publishing.

Frosty the Snowman

Rollins, J., Nelson, S. (1950). Chappell and Co.

Gaudete

Contiones, P. (1972). Alfred Publishing Company, Inc.

Go Tell It on the Mountain

Traditional (adapted by Work, J. W.). Public Domain.

God Rest Ye Merry, Gentlemen

Traditional. Public Domain.

Good King Wenceslas

Neale, J. M. (1853) Public Domain.

Happy Xmas (War Is Over)

Lennon, J., Ono, Y. (1971). Downtown Dmp Songs o.b.o. Lenono Music.

Hark! The Herald Angels Sing

Wesley, C. & Mendelssohn, F. (1739). Public Domain.

Have Yourself a Merry Little Christmas

Martin, H., Blane, R. (1947). EMI Feist Catalog Inc/ Redcoats Are Coming Publishing/Universal Music - Brentwood Benson Songs (Gotee).

I Saw Three Ships

Traditional. Public domain.

I Wish It Could Be Christmas Everyday

Wood, R. (1973). Anne-Rachel Music and EMI April Music Inc.

In Dulci Jubilo

Traditional. Public domain.

In the Bleak Midwinter

Rossetti, C. (1872). Public Domain.

It Came Upon the Midnight Clear
> Sears, E. (1849). Public Domain.

It's Beginning to Look a Lot Like Christmas
> Willson, M. (1951). Kobalt Music Pub America Inc. o.b.o.
> Frank-Meredith Willson Music

It's the Most Wonderful Time of the Year
> Pola, E., Wyle, G. (1963). Barnaby Music Corp. c/o Songs
> of Peer, Ltd. Barnaby Music Corp.

Jingle Bell Rock
> Beal, J., Boothe, J. (1957). Chappell and Co.

Jingle Bells
> Pierpont, J. L. (1850). Public Domain.

Joy to the World
> Watts, I. (1719). Public Domain.

Last Christmas
> Michael, G. (1984). London: Warner Chappell Production
> Music.

Let It Snow! Let It Snow! Let It Snow!
> Cahn, S. and Styne, J. EMI Feist Catalog Inc.

Lonely This Christmas
> Chapman, M., Chinn, N. (1974). Universal Music Mgb
> Songs.

Mary, Did You Know?
> Lowry, M., Greene, B. (1984/1991). Capitol Cmg Genesis
> o.b.o. Rufus Music and Word Music, Inc.

Mary's Boy Child
Hairston, J. (1956). Schumann Music Co.

Merry Xmas Everybody
Rundquist, S., A., Olsen, S, A., Holder, N., Lea, J. (1980). Barn Publishing Ltd.

Mistletoe and Wine
Strachan, K., Paul, J., Stewart, L., G. (1988). BMG Bumblebee o.b.o. Patch Music.

O Come, All Ye Faithful
Traditional. Public Domain.

O Come, O Come, Emmanuel
Traditional. Public Domain.

O Holy Night
Cappeau, P. (1843) Public Domain.

O Little Town of Bethlehem
Brooks, P. & Redner, L. H. (1868). Public Domain.

O Tannenbaum (O Christmas Tree)
Traditional. Public Domain.

Once in Royal David's City
Alexander, C. F. & Gauntlett, H. (1848). Public Domain.

Peace on Earth/Little Drummer Boy
Kohan, B. Fraser, I., Grossman, L. (1977). Published by – Chappell Music Ltd. Bewlay Bros. Music. Fleur Music Ltd. E.G. Music Ltd. Kennicott-David, K., Onorati, H., Simeone, H. (1941). Holly Music Group.

Rockin' around the Christmas Tree
Marks, J. (1958). St. Nicholas Music Inc.

Rudolph the Red-Nosed Reindeer
Marks, J. (1964). St. Nicholas Music Inc.

Santa Claus Is Comin' to Town
Coots F., Gillespie, H. (1994). Haven Gillespie Music Pub. Co. and Wixen Music Publishing o.b.o Toy Town Tunes, Inc.

Silent Night
Gruber, F. X. and Mohr, J. (1818). Public Domain.

Sleigh Ride
Anderson, L., Parish, M. (1948). EMI Mills Music Inc. and BMG Gold Songs o.b.o Woodbury Music Co.

Stay Another Day
Hawken, D., Kean, R., Mortimer, A. (1994). Universal - Songs of Polygram International, Inc. Porky Publishing and BMG Platinum Songs o.b.o Bandmodel Ltd.

Step into Christmas
John, E., Taupin, B. (1973). Universal – Songs of Polygram International Inc.

The Twelve Days of Christmas
Traditional. Public Domain.

The Christmas Song
Wells, R., Torme, M. (1945). Edwin H. Morris & Co/Edwin H. Morris & Co./Edwin H. Morris & Co. (A Div. Of MPL

Music Publishing, Inc.)/Edwin H. Morris & Co. A Div Of MPL Communications/KOBALT Music Pub America I o.b.o. Edwin H Morris & Co/KOBALT Music Pub America I o.b.o. Edwin H. Morris & Company/Sony ATV Tunes, LLC o.b.o. Aggressive Music (Hfa)/Sony/ATV Songs LLC/ Sony/ATV Tunes/Sony/ATV Tunes LLC/Sony/ATV Tunes LLC/Sony/ATV Tunes, LLC DBA ATV o.b.o. ATV (Northern Songs Catalog).

The First Noel
Traditional. Public Domain.

The Holly and the Ivy
Traditional. Public Domain.

The Little Drummer Boy
Kennicott-David, K., Onorati, H., Simeone, H. (1941). Holly Music Group.

This Christmas
Hathaway, D., McKinnor, N. (1970). California, Santa Monica: Universal Music Group.

Walking in the Air
Blake, H. (1982). G. Schirmer, Inc. o.b.o. Highbridge Music Ltd.

We Three Kings
Hopkins, J. H. (1857). Public Domain.

We Wish You a Merry Christmas
Traditional. Public Domain.

When a Child Is Born

    Jacobson, F., Dammicco, C. (1970). Beechwood Music Corp.

White Christmas

    Berlin, I. (1940). New York, NY: Irving Berlin Music Company.

Winter Wonderland

    Bernard, F., Smith, D. (1934). WB Music Corp.

Wonderful Christmastime

    McCartney, P. (2017). Mpl Communications Inc.

100 BEST CHRISTMAS POEMS FOR CHILDREN

Edited by
Roger McGough

Also available
ISBN 9780281084692